JN412036

THE ESSENCE OF WRITING 2

GENRE-BASED APPROACH

이 도서는 2017학년도 한국외국어대학교 HUFS특성화 사업의 일환으로 출판된 도서입니다.

대학필수 영작문

THE ESSENCE OF WRITING 2

GENRE-BASED APPROACH

장르별 실용 영작문

최호성 · 유호정 · 이진환 공저

Alice Julianna Yoo · Brian Hupman 영문 감수

HU:iNE

Preface

This book is designed to help non-native English speakers communicate their thoughts effectively in English by practicing and mastering writing skills needed in real-life situations. To achieve this goal, we selected five genres that are used most frequently in our everyday lives, and contained writing skills and useful expressions with specific and practical examples in each unit.

With this idea in mind, *the Essence of Writing 2: Genre-based Approach*, one of the sequels for L2 writing that we co-projected, has been made. Students could learn the essence of more academic writing by using infographics to visualize information in the first book, *the Essence of Writing 1: Paragraphs with Infographics*, whereas they will be able to master the core of more practical writing in the second book.

This book is composed of five essential units and three practical appendices. In addition to the fundamental genre-based studies, *Writing Tips* and *Writing Templates* in each unit are also helpful to learners in practicing grammatically correct and explicit sentences.

"What is written without effort is in general read without pleasure," said Samuel Johnson. While words once spoken can never be recalled, fortunately, we can revise our manuscripts again and again. We hope this book, *the Essence of Writing 2: Genre-based Approach*, will be a clear and useful guide for both teachers and learners.

Contents

Appendices

Answer Key

Introduction

"Language is a mirror of the mind."

— *Noam Chomsky*

"The limits of my language
are the limits of my world."

— *Ludwig Josef Johann Wittgenstein*

Writing Through Genres

What is genre? It comes straight from French, literally meaning "a kind." Genre is a particular style or category of literature, art, or music. What are some book genres? The two main categories separating the different genres of books are fiction and nonfiction. When we focus on writing itself, the basic ones, which are often used in the classroom, are narrative, descriptive, argumentative, and expository. There could be more genres because different people define the genres of writing differently. For instance, email writing, text messaging, newsletters, travel writing, and cover letters could be recognized as different genres. All of these genres are associated with specific features and functions that distinguish them from one another.

We use email for communication with family, relatives, friends, and colleagues. It is a very simple and easy communication tool used throughout our daily lives. But, only a few people think that email is a genre of writing, because most people regard email as talking rather than writing. However, email writing is a discrete genre and should be identified as such. We use email for all kinds of purposes such as job applications and business marketing. There are also email etiquette rules that we should abide by. Text messaging is meant to be focused and succinct, because single text messages are limited to 160 characters including spaces. Long messages are not recommended at all. People use social networking services such as Twitter, Facebook, Instagram, and mobile messengers like KakaoTalk to build social networks and share their interests with others. When you write a social media post, you should keep in mind that it can be public whether you want it to be or not.

Since a newsletter is considered a way to sell or advertise products and periodically deliver information, people tend to neglect it. It can be a valuable marketing tool, but it is different from an advertisement in nature. A newsletter's content is highly reliable, unique, and interesting, which needs to be related to marketing to some degree. Travel writing, also known as travelogue and itinerary, is a popular literary genre where descriptive accounts abound. A travel description can be a very useful tool to reach out to potential travelers. It needs to attract them to the places you describe, as well as offer precise information for them not to waste time and money. Cover letters are a genre that has evolved from job application letters. Cover letters are very professional, formal letters, and simultaneously they should be appealing and eye catching for employment. For you to make a great impression on the person who may hire you, you should also understand the essential elements of a strong cover letter. Do not forget that the stronger your cover letter is, the more job interview opportunities you will have!

Unit 1

E-mail

Objectives

- To identify the basic format of e-mails
- To learn the contents and customary expressions based on the purpose of a given email
- To understand and practice the writing rules of fragments, comma splices, and run-ons
- To understand and practice the grammar rules of finite and nonfinite verbs

"Email may well be your most productive marketing tool."

— *Dan Zarrella*

"Like almost everyone who uses e-mail,
I receive a ton of spam every day.
Much of it offers to help me get out of
debt or get rich quick.
It would be funny if it weren't so exciting."

— *Bill Gates*

Warm-up Activity

Writing Model

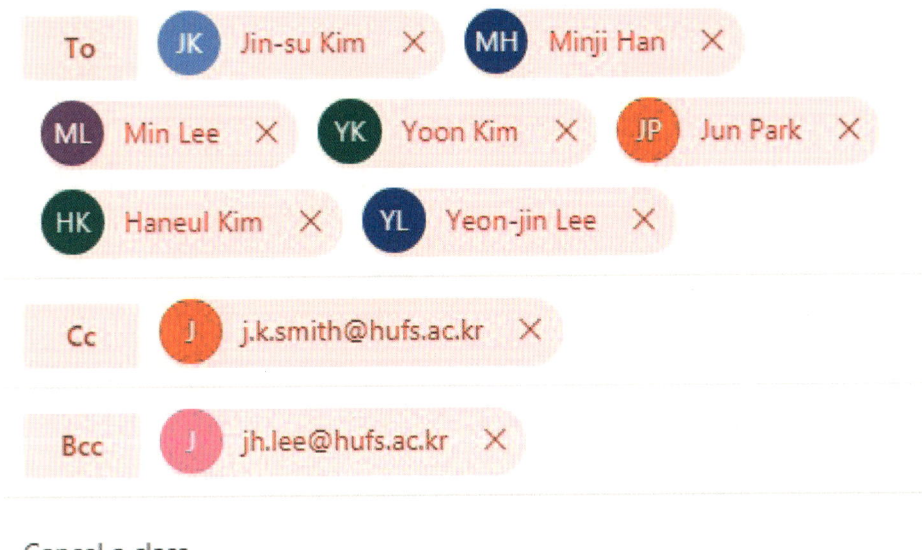

Cancel a class

Class students,

Prof. Smith wanted me to inform you all that next week's class has been canceled since he will go abroad to attend a conference. The class will be rescheduled soon. Once Mr. Smith advises me of the new class time, I'll send you another email. Please note that you have to do your weekly scheduled assignments according to the syllabus.

Regards,

Ye-won Lee
Teaching Assistant, The Faculty of Liberal Arts

What is an E-mail?

E-mail, an abbreviation of *electronic mail*, is a method of exchanging written messages between people electronically. In other words, e-mail is a system of world-wide electronic communication in which a computer user can compose a message at one terminal that can be regenerated at the recipient's terminal when the recipient logs in.

E-mail first entered substantial use in the 1960s and by the mid-1970s had taken on the form now recognized as e-mail. E-mail operates across computer networks, which today is primarily the Internet. Some early e-mail systems required the author and the recipient to both be online at the same time, similar to some instant messaging services. Today's e-mail systems are based on a store-and-forward model. E-mail servers accept, forward, deliver, and store messages. Neither the users nor their computers are required to be online simultaneously; they need to connect only briefly, typically to a mail server or a webmail interface, for as long as it takes to send or receive messages.

Now, let's identify the basic format and the customary expressions of an e-mail.

The format of email

① Addressee	To: *******@naver.com Cc: *******@hanmail.net Bcc: *******@hufs.ac.kr
② Subject	Re:
③ Attachment	
④ Greeting	
⑤ Text	the body
⑥ Closing	
⑦ Sender	

① Addressee: Who you are sending your email to.
- To: addressee
- Cc (= Carbon Copy): '*cc*' is used to indicate that a copy is being sent to another person.
- Bcc (= Blind Carbon Copy): '*bcc*' is used to imply that a duplicate is being sent to another person without the knowledge of the main recipient.

② Subject: What your email is about.

- Re: '*Re*' may be used in business letters, faxes, or other official documents to introduce a subject to be discussed meaning "regarding" or "in regards to."

  (cf. In most everyday emails, however, it may simply mean "reply," or that you are replying to an email that had previously been sent to you.)

③ Attachment: This is a file which is added separately to a message that you send to someone.

④ Greeting: How you will address the person or people you are writing to.

Formal style	Dear Mr./Mrs./Miss/Ms. + Last name
	Dear Sir/Madam/Sir or Madam: To whom it may concern:
Informal style	Dear + First name Hi + First name

⑤ Text: This is the main body of your email.

⑥ Closing: This is your closing salutation, or how you will say goodbye.

Formal style	Sincerely (yours), Yours sincerely, Cordially (yours), Yours cordially,
Informal style	Regards, Best regards/wishes, With best wishes, Yours truly,
	Best, Love, Yours, Warmly,

⑦ Sender: If necessary, you can contain your signature.

Write a thank-you letter to someone by e-mail.

To:
From:
Date:
Subject:

Writing Checklist: E-mail

As you write your e-mail, review the checklist below and ask yourself the following questions.

- ✔ I observed the basic email formatting rules.
- ✔ I applied customary expressions to the e-mail.
- ✔ I used relevant expressions on the topic.

Practice 1

Judge the correct expression of following sentences with T(true) or F(false).

1. '*Cc:*' is used to indicate that a copy is being sent to another person. (   )
2. '*Re*' is used only to indicate to reply to someone's letter in business letters, faxes, or other official documents. (   )
3. The word, *snail mail*, is used especially to describe the system of sending letters by ordinary mail because it is very slow in comparison with e-mail. (   )

Writing Drills

Writing an E-mail is far more convenient than mailing a letter in an envelope. It is sometimes even more so than using the telephone. By using email to invite, request, purchase, or complain about something, you may speed up the business handling process and make your business communications simplified and efficient.
E-mails can be divided into different parts depending on their purpose. In this unit, you will learn and practice everyday-related e-mails and business-related e-mails.

Part A. Everyday-related E-mails

In part A, you will be able to learn and practice everyday-related e-mails, such as greetings, introductions, invitations, requests and notices. Keep in mind, it is especially important that you use apt expressions for each situation based on who you are writing to and the contents.

Writing Model

To: keller99@personalmail.com

From: maintenance@hufshill-apartments.com

Date: September 12

Subject: Safety Check

Dear Mr. Keller,

I am writing to remind you of our regular safety inspection. Each year, we at Hufshill Apartments conduct safety checks for each unit in the building. Yours is scheduled for Saturday, September 22, at 4:30 P.M. The process will take approximately one hour to complete. Please note that the inspection cannot be performed unless you are present for the check, so if this appointment time does not work for you, let me know as soon as possible. I will then reschedule you for another date or time.
The inspection will consist of checking the lights, plumbing, appliances, and water leaks. If the maintenance workers find any minor problems, they will fix them. Upgrades will also be made if necessary. If you are aware of any problems in your unit, please let them know upon arrival.

Regards,
Jim Johnson
Hufshill Apartments

Questions about the Model

1. Why was the email sent to Mr. Keller?

2. What is Mr. Keller asked to do on September 22nd, at the time of inspection?

Useful Expressions

Write other useful expressions fitting the titles.

A. Greeting

- It's been far too long since I wrote you.
- What have you been up to lately?
- How is your family? I trust your family is well.

B. Introduction

- I'd like to introduce myself. I am a freshman, Jin-su Kim.
- My name is James Bond and I am the departmental student representative.
- It's a pleasure to know a nice professor like you.

C. Invitation

- Are you free on Friday to join us for dinner?
- Would you like to join us for a drink this weekend?
- We are pleased to offer you an invitation to our upcoming seminar.

D. Request

- I'm writing to ask you a favor. Can you meet me at the airport?
- I'm sorry to say I can't help you with it.
- The situation has worsened in recent years. What do you think I should do?

E. Notice

- We are happy to announce the engagement of our daughter.
- I'm happy to announce that you are our employee of the month.
- I have some great news for you.

Brainstorming

Write an everyday-related e-mail to someone with reference to the following topics.

- ✔ an email to a friend about a lunch date
- ✔ an invitation email to your friend to go on a trip
- ✔ a request email to your teacher to extend your project deadline

Draft

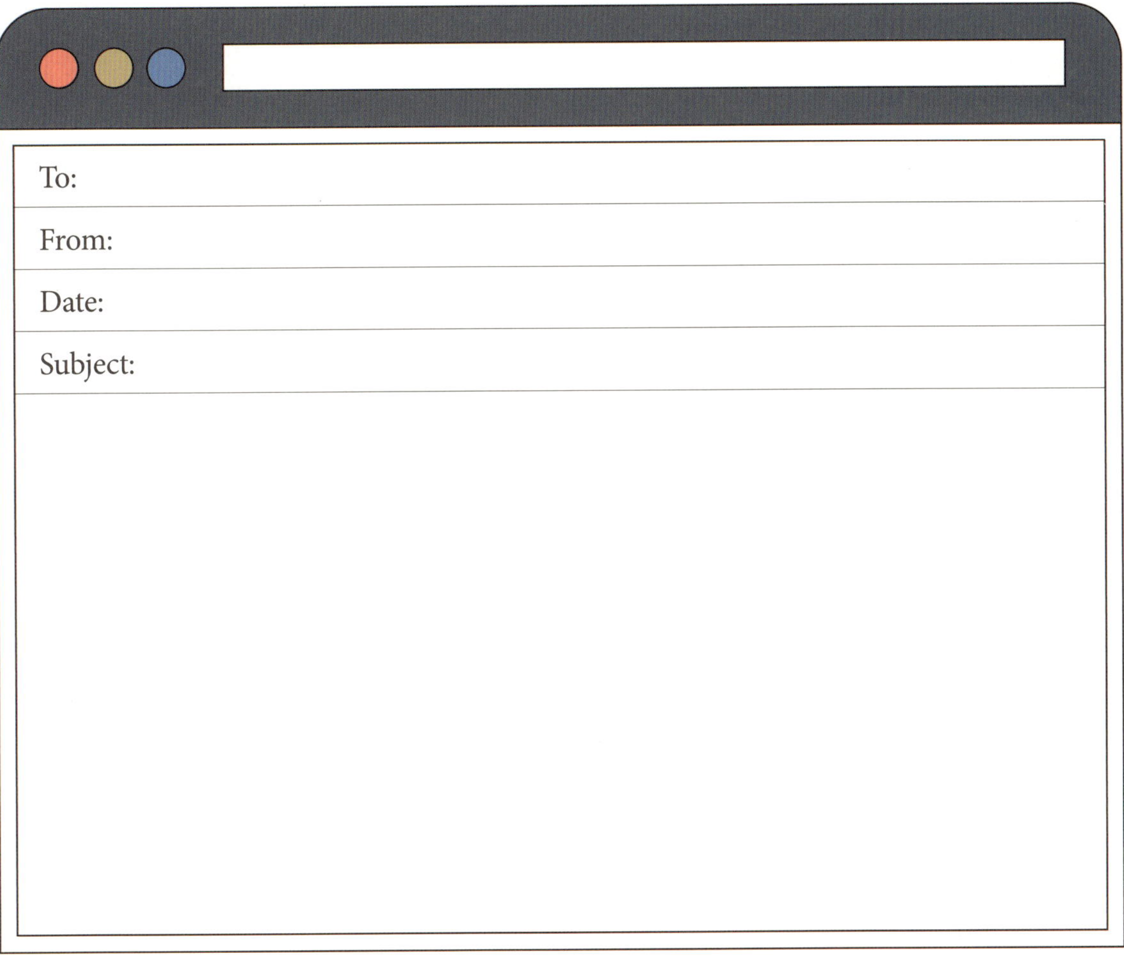

Peer feedback

Part B. Business-related E-mails

In part B, you will be able to learn and practice writing about different points used in business-related e-mails, such as company/product introductions, making purchases, negotiations, payments, and delivery. Depending on the purpose and intention of the e-mail, you need to use appropriate expressions for each situation.

Writing Model

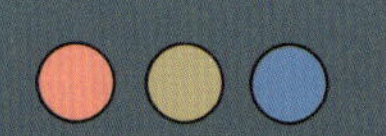

To: customerservice@smartsupplies.com

From: sjohnson99@hannaver.net

Date: September 6

Subject: Purchase

To Whom It May Concern,

Last month, I made a purchase on my credit card from your DIY store, but I believe a mistake was made. I ordered a shelf over the telephone and was charged $77.00 despite the fact that the item was on sale for $70.00. Even though you normally charge $10.00 for shipping, I took advantage of your special offer that stated all customers who spent $3.00 or more would receive free shipping. Therefore, I would appreciate it if you refund me the amount of money that was overcharged. I hope the issue can be resolved quickly, and I look forward to doing more business wish you in the future.

Respectfully yours,

Samuel Johnson

Questions about the Model

1. What is the purpose of Mr. Johnson's email?

2. What is the meaning of the word, *DIY*?

3. What line of business is the company, Smartsupplies?

Useful Expressions

Write other useful expressions fitting the titles.

A. Company/Product Introduction

- We are happy to announce the release of our new product.
- Our smartphones use the latest technology, but are reasonably priced.
- Our insurance company has branches that cover residential properties in Yongin-si.
- ______________________________

B. Purchasing

- We are confirming the order you placed yesterday.
- I'm placing an order for stationery. Is there anything you need?
- You can purchase *The Essence of Writing 2* from an online bookstore.
- ______________________________

C. Negotiation

- I will contact you after I review your proposal.
- We hope you reconsider your decision regarding our proposal.
- What is the lowest fare you can give me for a return flight to Seoul, leaving before the 24th?
- ______________________________

D. Payment

- How can I pay my bills?
- The payment has been made to your account.
- If you pay by cash, we can offer you a 5% discount on the order.
- ______________________________

E. Delivery

- The shipping and handling (fee) is free.
- Is the delivery charge included in the price?
- When and how will the package be delivered?
- ______________________________

Brainstorming

Write a business-related e-mail to an imaginary company with reference to the following topics.

- ✔ a complaint about a shipping delay
- ✔ an e-mail explaining the return of a purchased product for a refund
- ✔ negotiating a better price for the products you would like to purchase

Draft

To:

From:

Date:

Subject:

Peer feedback

Writing Tips

A. Writing Skills: Fragments, Comma Splices, and Run-ons

- **Fragments:** Every sentence must have at least a subject and a verb to express a complete idea. If you leave out either the subject or the verb, your sentence is incomplete. This is called a fragment.

  a. *Like to shop quickly.
  b. *Most men to shop quickly.
  c. Most men like to shop quickly.

  cf. the asterisk mark(*) means that the sentence is grammatically incorrect.

- **Comma splices:** To link two or more independent clauses in a sentence, a conjunction, colon, or semicolon should be used. If you join two clauses by using just a comma, your sentence is incomplete. This is called a comma splice or comma fault.

  a. *John likes to shop quickly, Jane likes to take her time.
  b. John likes to shop quickly, but Jane likes to take her time.
  c. John likes to shop quickly; however, Jane likes to take her time.

- **Run-ons:** If you contain two or more independent clauses without appropriate punctuation in a sentence, your sentence is incomplete. This is called a run-on.

  a. *John likes to shop quickly Jane likes to take her time.
  b. John likes to shop quickly. Jane likes to take her time.
  c. While John likes to shop quickly, Jane likes to take her time.

Practice 2 Read each sentence. Then correct each sentence in any way possible.

1. The long summer vacation has just ended I wait the day of winter vacation.
   - ....
   - ....

2. The sentence errors include fragments comma splices and run-ons.
   - ....
   - ....

B. Grammar Skills: Verb Tense; Finite Verbs vs. Nonfinite Verbs

Every sentence has a tense which exists within a verb phrase. A finite verb is a verb that carries a tense, whereas a nonfinite verb is a verb that doesn't carry any tense. (cf. Don't confuse the verb tense with the sentence tense. ☞ p.46)

- **Finite verbs**: Finite verb forms occur either in the present tense or in the past tense.

(1) The present tense is **base form** and *—s* **form** (in 3rd person singular present tense).

a. I keep a diary every day.

b. Min-ho sometimes keeps a diary.

c. He is keeping a diary in his room.

(2) The past tense

a. Su-ji kept a diary when she was an elementary school student.

b. She had kept a diary for six years.

- **Nonfinite verbs**: Nonfinite verb forms are found in four types.

(1) bare infinitive

a. I must keep a diary every day.

b. The teacher had me keep a diary every day.

(2) *to*-infinitive

a. Middle school students do not want to keep a diary.

(3) present participle

a. He is keeping a diary in his room.

(4) past participle

a. She had kept a diary for six years.

Practice 3 Judge the grammaticality of the underlined words in the following sentences with F(finite) or N(nonfinite).

1. He had been keeping a diary for 12 years. (F / N)
2. He had been keeping a diary for 12 years. (F / N)
3. He had been keeping a diary for 12 years. (F / N)

C. Collocation Drills by Subjects

Select one of the words in parenthesis to complete the sentence.

(1) Everyday-related e-mail expressions

- I'm sorry I didn't respond (early / earlier) to your e-mail.
- When should I schedule a (after / follow-up) visit?
- Please find the (attaching / attached) minutes of yesterday's meeting.
- Thank you for your (interest / interesting) in booking a room.
- My mother began her teaching (career / job) in a high school.
- Be careful not to (make / take) a mistake like that again.
- I think he needs to learn (hand / cellular) phone etiquette.
- We are endeavoring to (make / raise) a fund for the poor and homeless.
- Most of us use (general / public) transport to get to schools or companies.
- The mass media plays a crucial role in (building / forming) public opinion.

(2) Business-related e-mails expressions

- Advertising (pay / revenue) is increasing every year.
- I'm (attaching / detaching) the detailed specifications of the product.
- Would you send me a (comprehensible / comprehensive) list of your prices?
- Could you please (calculate / evaluate) the shipping charges?
- I'm writing to complain (about / to) the state of the rooms.
- Mr. Kim is no longer with our company; I am his (replacement / replenishment).
- It's not a good idea for you to (negate / neglect) your office duties.
- We look forward to (build / building) a lasting business partnership in the future.
- Advantages to launching a startup in the city include a cheap (workforce / workout).
- We are an established company with a good reputation for building up (progressive / prosperous) businesses in a mechanical line.

Writing Assignments 1

Write a complete e-mail that is developed from one draft between the two previous writing drills.

Brainstorming

Outline

Final

To:

From:

Date:

Subject:

Writing Templates 1

{N: noun (phrase), to-V: to infinitive, S: subject, V: verb, that ~: that clause}

A. Interest

- I am interested in N.
- I have much[a wide] interests in N.
- I find X very interesting[exciting/intriguing/compelling].
- My main[particular] interest is to-V[that ~].
- S + interests[fascinates/intrigues] me very much[a great deal].

e.g.

a. I am very interested in the MBA courses offered at your school.

b. ______________________________

____

c. ______________________________

____

B. Intention

- I intend to-V.
- For[With] the purpose of N, S + V.
- With a view[an eye] to N, S + V.
- With the aim[intention] of N, S + V.
- The intention[purpose/aim/point/idea] of N is to V.
- Intentionally[Deliberately/Purposely/On purpose/By design], S + V.

e.g.

a. For the purpose of this research, a new method is under consideration.

b. ______________________________

____

c. ______________________________

____

C. Assertion

- I assert[contend/maintain/argue/insist] that ~.
- I am sure[certain/convinced/positive] that ~.

e.g.

a. I'm quite positive that the new policy will be much more effective than the previous one.

b. ______________________________

c. ______________________________

D. Opinion

- I think[believe] that ~.
- I have[hold/am of] the opinion that ~.
- My opinion[view] of the matter is that ~.
- In my opinion[view], S + V.
- From my[this/a moral/a commercial/an educational] point of view, S + V.

e.g.

a. In my opinion, your report needs a lot of corrections.

b. ______________________________

c. ______________________________

E. Proposal

- I propose[suggest/recommend/advise] that ~.
- My proposal[suggestion/idea] is that ~.
- What I propose[suggest] is to-V[that ~].

e.g.

a. I propose that we put it to a vote.

b. ______________________________

c. ______________________________

F. Generalization

- Generally[Broadly] (speaking), S + V.
- Largely[Mostly/On the whole/In general/By and large], S + V.
- In most cases[In a vast number of cases/In the majority of cases], S + V.
- I tend[am inclined/have a tendency] to-V.
- (Some) people say that ~.

e.g.

a. Generally speaking, getting enough sleep is involved in the body's immune system.

b. ______________________________

c. ______________________________

Unit 2

Text Messages and Comments

Objectives

- To identify the basic format of a text message and comment
- To learn useful abbreviations and expressions in text messages and comments
- To understand and practice the writing rules of unity and coherence
- To understand and practice the grammar rules of complex verb phrases

"Silence is a text easy to misread."

– *Alfred Angelo Attanasio*

"You have two ears and one mouth.
Follow that ratio.
Listen more, talk less."

– *Banksy*

"Happiness is
when what you think, what you say, and what you do
are in harmony."

– *Mahatma Gandhi*

Warm-up Activity

Writing Model

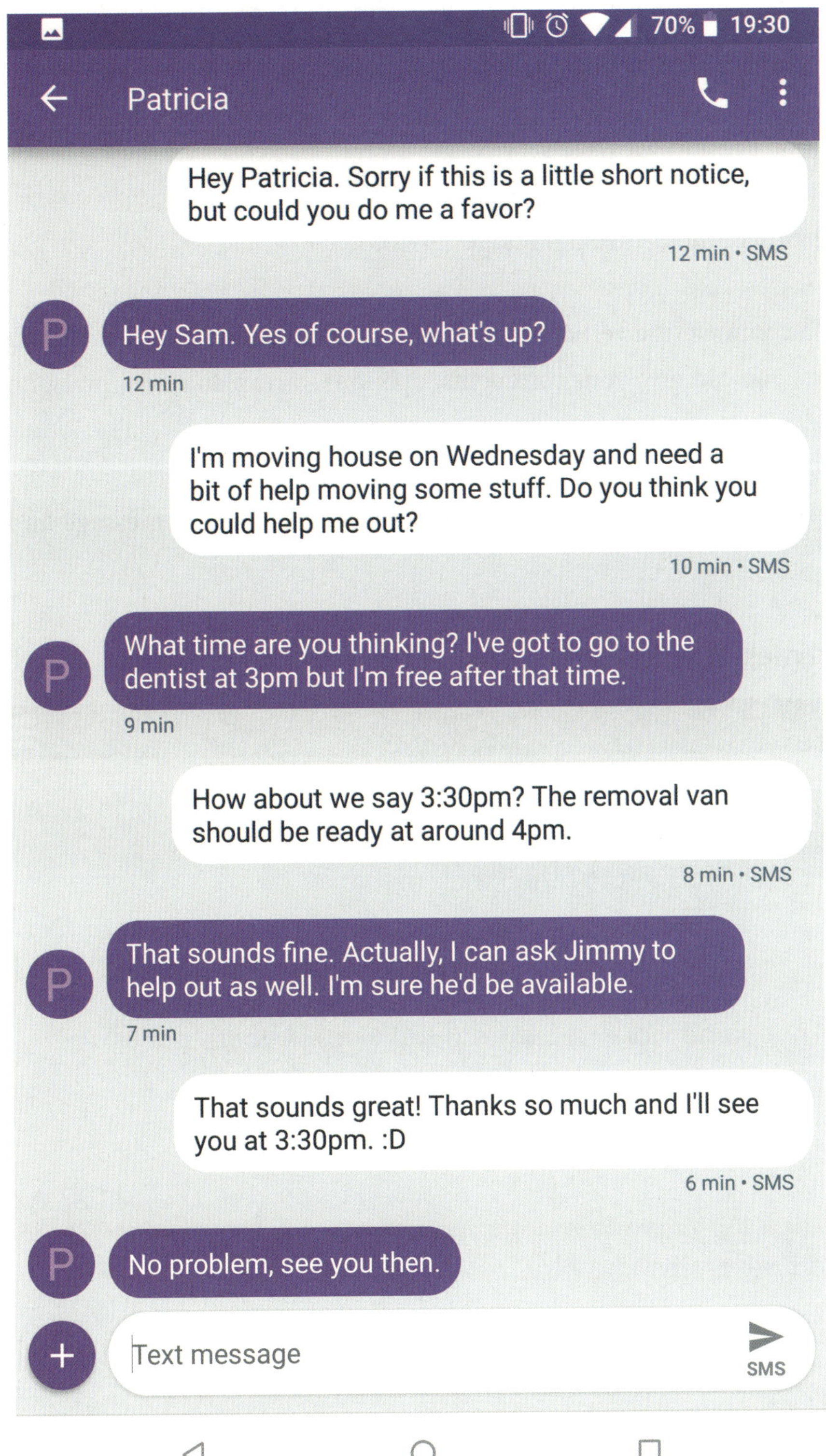

What is a Text Message and a Comment?

A text message is a type of electronic communication sent and received using a mobile phone. These days, computer and mobile users interact with other users through the use of dedicated websites and applications. Facebook, Instagram, and Kakaostory are typical examples of SNS, Social Networking Service, that help you find people with similar interests to your own. Based on length and contents we can see that there are three types of text messages.

- SMS is an abbreviation of Short Message Service
- LMS is an abbreviation of Long Message Service
- MMS is an abbreviation of Multi-media Message Service

Generally speaking, a comment is a verbal or written remark expressing one's own opinion or reaction. These days, you can give your comments, opinions, or explanations in response to a person's writings.

Now, let's identify the basic format and useful abbreviations of a text message and a comment.

The format of text message

① Alice ② 11:22 A.M.

③ Hey, Brian, have you left for the lunch meeting?

Brian 11:23 A.M.

Not yet. I've got some work to finish up right now. What's up?

(...)

Alice 11:27 A.M.

Got it! Do you need anything else?

Brian 11:28 A.M.

No, that's it. CU soon!

④ Send

① A message sender
② Sending time
③ Incoming or outgoing messages
④ Place to write your message to send

Useful chat abbreviations

abbr.	meaning	abbr.	meaning
Y	why	aka/a.k.a./AKA	also known as
UR	your	ASAP	as soon as possible
EZ	easy	ATM	at the moment
B4	before	HAND	have a nice day
PLS/plz	please	HBD	happy birthday
CUZ	because	IDC	I don't care
bro	brother	IDK/dunno	I don't know
sis	sister	KISS	keep it simple, stupid
bf	boyfriend	LTNS	long time no see
gf	girlfriend	OMG	oh my god
IC	I see	OTOH	on the other hand
CU	see you	POV	point of view
L8R	later	THX	thank you
F2F	face to face	TIA	thanks in advance
IOU	I owe you	TMI	too much information
IOW	in other words	WFM	works for me
KMN	kill me now	WRT	with regard to
LMK	let me know	XOXO	hugs and kisses

Draft

Imagine that you and a classmate are sending text messages to each other. First, come up with a situation, and then fill in the blanks using appropriate abbreviations from the prior list.

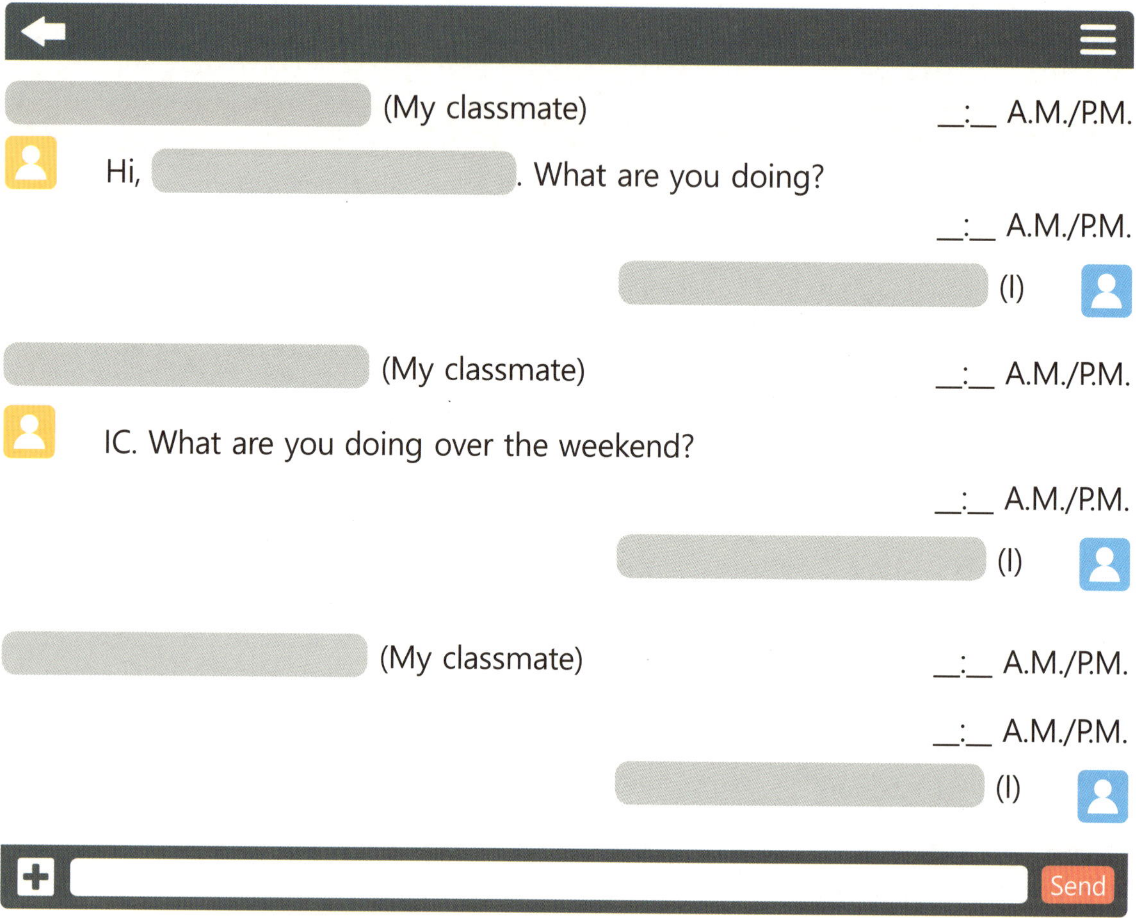

Writing Checklist: Text Messages and Comments

As you send a message or write a comment, review the checklist below and ask yourself the following questions.

- ✔ Did I observe the basic formatting rules of SMS and comments?
- ✔ Did I use appropriate abbreviations and acronyms in my writing?
- ✔ Did I use concise, polite, and reasonable expressions?

Practice 1

Judge whether the meanings of the following abbreviations are T(true) or F(false).

1. MMS is an abbreviation of Multi-media Message Service ( )
2. The chat abbreviation, XOXO, means 'hugs and kisses' ( )

Writing Drills

Part A. Text Messages

In part A, you will learn about and practice writing short text messages. SMS can be useful for you to send urgent messages to your friends or family members. Always, make an effort to express your ideas clearly and concisely.

Writing Model

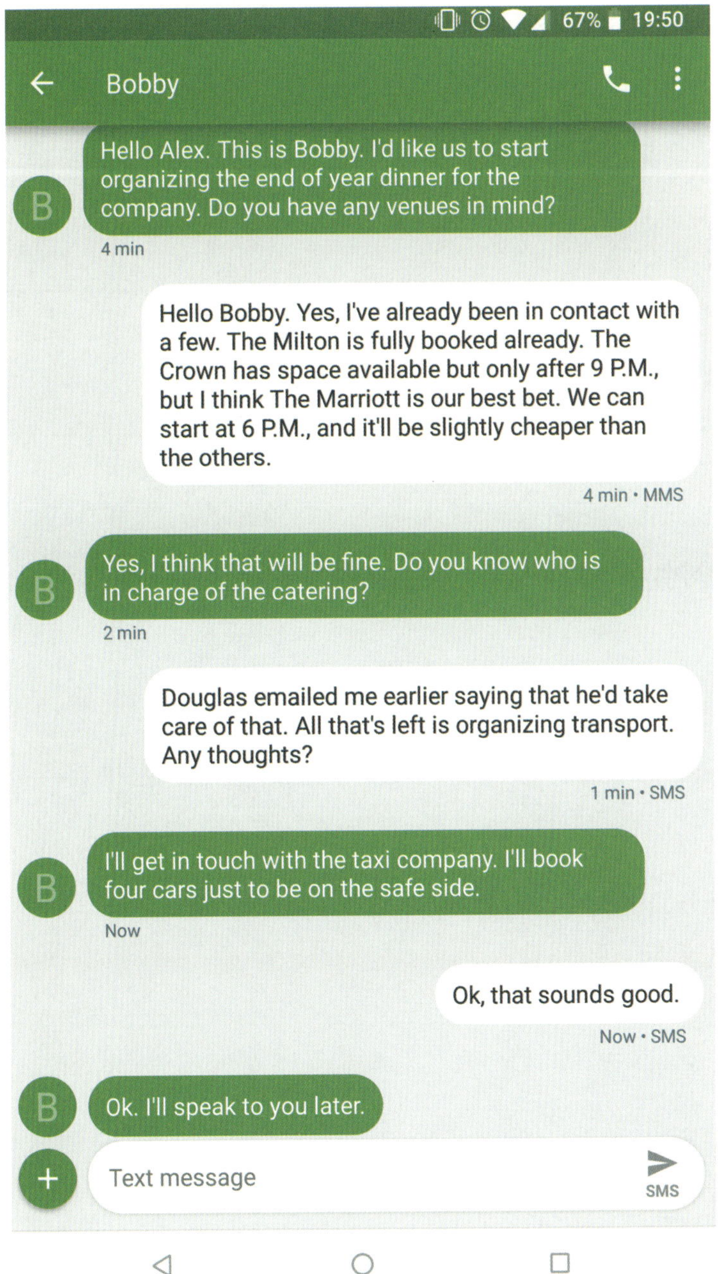

Questions about the Model

1. Who is going to arrange the catering for the event?

2. What kind of transportation will the attendees use?

Useful Expressions

Write other useful expressions fitting the titles.

A.

- BRB = be right back (BBL = be back later)
- BFN = bye for now
- BTW = by the way
- FAQ =
- FYI =
- JK =
- IMO =
- LMAO = laugh my ass off

e.g.

a. BTW, I personally don't like speech.

b.

B.

- LOL =
- OIC = oh I see
- OTP =
- ROTFL = rolling on the floor laughing
- SMH = shake my head
- TBH =
- TTYL =
- WTH = what the hell

e.g.

a. LOL, that's totally awesome!

b.

Brainstorming

Write an imaginary SMS with reference to one of the following topics.

- ✔ Speaking with a classmate about a class assignment
- ✔ Talking with a friend about lunch
- ✔ Chatting with a friend about what happened on the weekend

Draft

__:__ A.M./P.M.

__:__ A.M./P.M.

__:__ A.M./P.M.

__:__ A.M./P.M.

__:__ A.M./P.M.

__:__ A.M./P.M.

Send

Peer feedback

Part B. Comments

In part B, you will learn about and practice writing notes about an event in the news or a written discussion based on someone or something. Due to the increase of smart phone and internet usage, comments are now commonplace and frequently used. Since people may comment from all over the globe, it is important to understand colloquial expressions and how to use them appropriately to make intended comments.

Writing Model

I don't mean to bother you but could I get your signature please?

SmylesFrowns 5 points · 4 hours ago
P-UPS, business man's best friend and loyal companion
Reply Share Report Save Give gold

Stumplestiltzkin 3 points · 4 hours ago
United Puppy Service
Reply Share Report Save Give gold

Slothkitty 1 point · 2 hours ago
United Pupper Service, lol
Reply Share Report Save Give gold

TheLimeMayWin 2 points · 4 hours ago
He better not ruff up my package!
Reply Share Report Save Give gold

Useful colloquial expressions

24/7	I bet	You know what I mean?
Hang on.	I doubt it.	No problem. / Never mind.
No doubt.	I got it.	Don't let me down.
Sure thing.	I'm in.	Give it a try/go. (= Try your luck.)
What's up?	I'm on it.	That'll work.
Lighten up.	I'm on my way.	It's not my cup of tea.
It's close by.	I just got off.	Buzz off.
It's on me.	I need a ride.	My way or the highway.
You deserve it.	So is mine.	Beats the heck out of me. (BTHOOM)

Useful Expressions

Write other useful colloquial expressions that are frequently used in SMS and comments.

A.

- Can you do me a favor?
- Come up with an idea.
- Could we push back our meeting?
- Don’t worry about that.
- I don't think I can make it.
- I’ll catch up with you.
- I’ll let you know.
- I’m not following you.
- ______________________________
- ______________________________
- ______________________________

B.

- I’m not available all afternoon.
- I’m off now (= (I’ve) got to go. = GTG)
- It’s your call. (= It’s up to you.)
- I wish I could help you.
- Keep me updated/posted.
- Let me figure/check it out.
- Sorry, I’m getting late.
- Where are you heading?
- ______________________________
- ______________________________
- ______________________________

Like

Love

Haha

Wow

Sad

Angry

Brainstorming

Read the following news article. Then practice writing appropriate comments below.

NEWS DESK

Student Counseling Center Uses Fine Art to Counsel Students

In May, the Student Counseling Center set up a fine art therapy program to help students deal with their stress. Students participated in drawing activities such as their most recent feelings and traumatic memories.

The counseling center pinpoints that the stress comes from unknown mixed feelings such as depression and anger. "By analyzing what feelings they have, students get to know themselves. This helps them realize what causes the feeling of irritation," said Song Eun-ju, the counseling director.

Draft

Comment 1

Comment 2

Comment 3

Peer feedback

Writing Tips

A. Writing Skills: Unity and Coherence

- **Unity:** To write effectively, your writing must have unity (≒ focus). A paragraph with unity develops just one main idea and links it to the rest of your writing. Unity occurs when all of the ideas in your writing support each other. To achieve unity, you have to look at each supporting sentence with care and determine whether they support the topic sentence.

- **Coherence:** To write logically, your writing must have coherence(≒ logic). A paragraph with coherence flows logically from the beginning to the end. In other words, the flow of the sentences is smooth and the logical relationships among sentences must be clear. To achieve coherence, you have to use transition signals, synonyms, and pro-forms like pronouns, parallel forms, and logical order.
(cf. Refer to the *Appendix A. Connectors and Transitions.*)

Especially, transition expressions allow your sentences to flow smoothly, showing the logical relationships between sentences.

a. I enjoy sending text messages. **However**, I don't like writing e-mails.
b. I enjoy sending text messages, I don't like writing e-mails, **however**.

Practice 2 Complete the following sentences by selecting the most suitable words.

1. E-mails make it fun and convenient to get in touch with faraway friends and acquaintances. (Finally / For instance / Moreover), e-mails are free in essence.
2. The differences between the two might be subtle, (also / nevertheless / therefore) they do exist.
3. Formal writing requires proper organization, sophisticated words, and accurate grammar. (For example / In contrast / Therefore), SMS and comments can use abbreviations and slang.

B. Grammar Skills : Sentence Tense; Complex Verb Phrase

- **Tense, Aspect, and Voice:** Every verb phrase in a sentence must have '**tense**' and '**voice**', and can have '**aspect**.'

  a. He likes to swim in a 50m pool.
     (sentence tense: present, *likes* — a finite verb, *to swim* — a nonfinite verb)

  b. The stolen car was found in the vicinity of the station. (passive voice)

  c. The police found the missing vehicle in the vicinity of the station. (active voice)

  d. I have studied *The Essence of Writing* since March. (perfective aspect)

  e. It's been raining all day long. (progressive aspect)

- **Complex Verb Phrase:** In a complex verb phrase, the auxiliaries follow a strict order, and the finite verb tense occurs in the first verb of the complex verb phrase.

Modal ▷ Perfect ▷ Progressive ▷ Passive

```
will + bare-inf.
          have + p.p.
                   be + ~ing
                           be + p.p.
+)________________________________________
 will     have     been     being  p.p.
```

a. She was nominated for the Best Actress Award.

b. She is being nominated for the Best Actress Award this year.

c. She has been nominated for the Best Actress Award twice.

d. She has been being nominated for the Best Actress Award twice this year.

e. She will have been being nominated for the Best Actress Award twice this year.
   (Note. Structures like d. and e. are very rare in English.)

Practice 3 Judge the grammaticality of the underlined words in the following sentences by writing T(true) or F(false).

1. As had been forecast, it began to rain in the afternoon. ( )
2. The firm will have been taxed two times this year. ( )
3. The movie is having been nominated for the best film award twice this year. ( )

C. Collocation Drills by Subjects

Select one of the words in parenthesis to complete the sentence.

(1) Text messages

- FYI = for your (invitation / information)
- BTW = by the (way / week)
- JK = just (killing / kidding)
- FAQ = (finally / frequently) asked questions
- OTP = on the (payroll / phone)
- IOW = in (old / other) words
- WRT = with (regard / reminder) to
- That is okay as well from my (PO / POV).
- Hang (on / out). I'll be ready in a minute.
- Don't hesitate, just give it a (try / test).

(2) Comments

- It's (on / up) to you, it's your decision.
- Your opinion is important, (so / such) is mine.
- This is amazing. How did you (catch / come) up with an idea like that?
- You know, I (will / wish) I could help, but I can't.
- I'm not sure, it is (before / beyond) my understanding.
- Sad to say, my opinion is different (from / in) yours.
- It's hard to see what you're talking about. It doesn't (make / take) sense.
- I have no alternative but (accepting / to accept) your offer.
- Please put yourself in my (body / place), and then you can understand me.
- Thank you, but it's none of your (benefit / business). That's up to me to decide.

Writing Assignments 2

Write an imaginary SMS based on your draft in Writing Drills Part A.

Brainstorming

Outline

Final

__:__ A.M./P.M.

__:__ A.M./P.M.

__:__ A.M./P.M.

__:__ A.M./P.M.

__:__ A.M./P.M.

__:__ A.M./P.M.

Send

Writing Templates 2

{N: noun (phrase), to-V: to infinitive, S: subject, V: verb, that ~: that clause}

A. Classification

- There are several[three] kinds[sorts/types/classes] of N.
- I'd classify[divide/categorize] N into three [types/parts/kinds].
- S can be grouped[divided/classified/categorized] by date[subject/title].

e.g.

a. We can classify phonetics into three parts: acoustic, auditory, and articulatory phonetics.

b.

c.

B. Enumeration and Sequence

- First(ly), ~. Second(ly), ~. Third(ly), ~. Then[After this/Subsequently], ~. Finally[Lastly], ~.
- At[In] the first stage, ~. At[In] the second stage, ~. At[In] the third stage, ~. At[In] the next stage, ~. At[In] the last stage, ~.
- In the beginning, ~. Previously, ~. Then[Subsequently], ~. Later[Afterwards], ~. In the end, ~.
- Simultaneously[Coincidentally/At the same time], S + V.
- Soon [Shortly/Immediately/Before long/In the near future], S + V.

e.g.

a. In the near future, a four-day workweek may be possible.

b.

c.

C. Addition

- Also[Besides/Moreover/Additionally/Furthermore/In addition], S + V.
- In addition to X, S + V.

e.g.

a. In addition to English, he can speak Chinese.

b.

c.

D. Truth

- It is true that ~.
- Actually[Truly/Indeed/Honestly/In fact/In reality/As a matter of fact], S + V.
- Frankly speaking[To tell (you) the truth], S + V.
- Naturally[Of course], S + V.
- I am not sure[certain/convinced] about N[that ~].
- I doubt [wonder/suspect/don't know] if[whether] ~.
- There is surely some doubt about[as to] N.

e.g.

a. It is true that nature itself is a teacher and a school.

b.

c.

E. Regard

- Regarding[About/Concerning/As regards], S + V.
- With[in] regard[respect] to N, ~
- In relation to[In connection with] N, S + V.
- In this regard[respect/connection/context], S + V.
- As far as S is concerned, S + V.

e.g.

a. As far as I am concerned, I don't like your idea.

b.

c.

F. Alternative

- Alternatively[Otherwise/If not/On the other hand], S + V.
- Instead[On behalf/In place] of N, S + V.
- As an[another] opinion[alternative], S + V.

e.g.

a. Instead of waiving the entrance fee, the museum decided to receive donations from the visitors.

b.

c.

Add New Post
How I promote my new blog posts
How I promote my new blog posts

Unit 3

News Letters

Objectives
- To identify the basic purpose and types of newsletters
- To learn the useful words and expressions in newsletters
- To understand and practice the writing rules of concord and agreement
- To understand and practice the grammar rules of using the passive form

"From the beginning on,
newspapers have prospered for no reason:
giving readers the news that they want."

– Rupert Murdoch

"Hope doesn't come from calculating
whether the good news is winning out over the bad.
It's simply a choice to take action."

– Anna Lappe

Warm-up Activity

Writing Model

ABOUT US OPINION NEWS DESK CAMPUS NATIONAL CULTURE THEORY

NEWS DESK

HIMUN Discusses Int'l Order Amid Protectionism

▲ Attendees enjoy the 41st HIMUN general assembly.

HUFS International Model United Nations (HIMUN) and Korea International Trade Association (KITA) co-hosted the 41st HIMUN general assembly at Convention & Exhibition (COEX) auditorium on Aug. 6, providing students an opportunity to share ideas on the rise of protectionism policies.

The agenda for this year was "Seeking a new international order to cope with the rise of protectionism." Eleven undergraduate and graduate students from throughout the nation participated in the event as representatives.

First kicked off in 1958, the Model United Nations program is conducted based on the actual procedures adopted by the U.N.

By You Seo-yeon

2017.09.08 No : 488

What is a Newsletter?

A newsletter, issued periodically for the members of an organization or specific consumers, is a regular means of communication. The format of newsletters vary. For instance, it may be a printed letter, an e-mail, a leaflet, a newspaper, or a webpage. The tone of newsletters is an informal free style. However, the intention behind newsletters is always clear. The purpose is to build a long-term relationship among members and to give special information to the members or customers.

When you plan a newsletter, the most important aspect to consider is who your readers are. Before writing, you should check the information about your readers as shown in the list below.

- The type of occupation, position or status
- The matter of common interest
- The most convenient medium; by email? by smart phone?
- The time to spend reading your newsletter

Now, let's identify some samples and study the customary expressions of newsletters.

VOLUME 1 ISSUE 2

Employee Newsletter

Newsletter Date

Inside This Issue

1 Message from the President
2 Employee News
2 Department Profile
2 Industry News
3 Employee Profile
3 News from HR
4 Birthdays and Anniversaries
4 Upcoming Events

Excerpt text from the main text of a story to draw a reader's attention to the page.

Front Page Employee News

The purpose of a newsletter is to provide specialized information to a targeted audience. Employee newsletters can be used to develop a better informed workforce, to foster a greater sense of community, and to build morale.

You can create a better informed workforce in many ways. By providing news from the project level and the company level, you can help employees better understand how the company works and where they fit in.

When employees understand the goals of the company and see how their work helps to achieve those goals, they are usually more productive.

You can help build morale by writing about employee events and achievements.

The key to a successful newsletter is making it useful to your readers. Include information about all areas of the company - but make sure it is information that your readers want and need.

Message from the President

An employee newsletter is an excellent place for a message from the President of the company. This article serves several purposes. For the President, it offers a way to communicate the company goals and status to employees at all levels.

For employees, it provides a better understanding of the company's goals and status, as the President sees them. If you want to create a sense of connection between employees and the president, you can use this column as a forum wherein the President can answer questions sent in by employees.

This column is also a great way to inform employees of big company news before it hits the TV or major newspapers.

To make this column successful, you should ask the president to be as candid and honest as possible. This is a place to inform employees, not promote a project or sell an idea.

The Association of Real Estate Funds Monthly Newsletter

February 2015

AREF

Old Mutual Property Fund
180 West George Street, Glasgow

For all enquiries:
AREF
65 Kingsway
London WC2B 6TD
Email: info@aref.org.uk
Web: www.aref.org.uk
Tel: 020 7269 4677

European Long-term Investment Funds (ELTIFs)

The AREF Regulation Committee have written an article on the proposed regulation for the creation of a new authorised collective investment vehicle, known as European Long-term Investment Funds (ELTIFs). The article can be viewed on the AREF website (click here for link).

AREF and PFR Global Real Estate Funds Review H2 2014

The H2 2014 edition of this report is now available on the AREF website (click here for link). As part of our continued drive to increase transparency in the funds industry, this twice-yearly review commissioned from Property Funds Research (PFR) gives a comprehensive picture of the real estate funds market globally, using data gathered on nearly 1,000 funds worldwide.

Membership changes

- Palmer Capital have joined as Associate Members.

Committee Changes

- Chris Hills of Investec and Stephen Palmer of Alecta have joined Investor Committee.

ESG on AREF Website

AREF's Environmental & Social Governance Committee have prepared a new page on the AREF website, advising members on social and environmental issues. To view the page click here:
http://www.aref.org.uk/esg.

Pensions Charge Cap

New rules introduce a charge cap for auto enrolment default funds and place new reporting obligations on pensions trustees. The costs of property management will be taken into account in accessing compliance with the charge cap and this could affect default funds ability to allocate to property. Pensions trustees will be required to report transaction costs and comment on whether they are value for money.

AREF members will need to develop the capability to provide trustees with the information they require which will mean dissecting the PER to identify the transaction cost elements (such as letting and lease renewal costs) and the elements attributable to the charge cap. Trustees are likely to start requesting this information in H2 2015.

To tackle these issues, AREF is forming a small working group. Please volunteer if this is an area of interest to you.

Sponsored Event:

Estate Gazette
3rd Annual Residential Summit
21st - 22nd April 2015
at The Waldorf Hilton Hotel, London

Expert speaker line-up, explores:

- The political climate and the impact on the delivery of housing
- The land equation - where will new sites come from?
- Innovative ways of bringing investment into the market
- How will infrastructure influence the construction of new housing?

Click here for more information

Exclusive offer from AREF: Please click here and add the promo code YWR69808 to save £270* off.
For more details please contact: saniya.maralova@rbi.co.uk.

AREF Events

Wednesday 4 March 2015
8.30am
Presentation of AREF/IPD Quarterly UK Property Fund Index

Wednesday 1 April 2015
5.00pm onwards
'Fund Structures' Educational & Networking Event

Tuesday 2 June 2015
6.00pm onwards
AREF Members Summer Drinks Reception
at The Royal Exchange, EC3V 3DG

Wednesday 23 September
6.00pm onwards
AREF Annual Dinner & Awards 2015
at The Dorchester Hotel, Park Lane

Further details on our events can be found here:
http://www.aref.org.uk/events

For event enquiries or to register please email: info@aref.org.uk

Useful Words and Phrases

① University

Bachelor's (degree) [B.A. = Bachelor of Arts]
Master's (degree) [M.A. = Master of Arts] [MBA = Master of Business Administration]
Doctor's (degree) [Ph.D. = Doctor of Philosophy] [Honorary Doctorate]
Teaching Assistant (TA) [Research Assistant (RA)]
Professor [Full Professor, Associate Professor, Assistant Professor, Lecturer]
School of English for Interpretation and Translation
College of Interpretation and Translation
Foreign Language Education Center (FLEC)
Academic Committee on General Course
Dormitory [Hall of Residence]
Office of Academic Affairs [Dean of Academic Affairs]
Hankuk University of Foreign Studies [President of HUFS]

② Company

Staff [Assistant, Associate, Assistant Manager]
Coworker(= Colleague), Subordinate, (Immediate) Supervisor
Team Leader [Manager, Head, Senior Manager, General Manager]
Director [Managing Director, Executive Director]
President [Vice President, CEO = Chief Executive Officer]
Headquarters [Head Office]
Branch Office, Subsidiary, affiliate
Company(Co.), Corporation(Corp.), Incorporated(Inc.) [Firm, Business]
Human Resources Department (= HR Department)
Public Relation Department (= PR Department = Publicity Department)
Customer Service Department
Accounting/Maintenance/Marketing/Sales/Shipping Department

Draft

Suppose you contribute to a school newsletter. Write a brief article to publicize your club or department.

Title:

Writing Checklist: Newsletters

As you write a newsletter, review the checklist below and ask yourself the following questions.

✔ Did I check the considerations of the readers?
✔ Did I use appropriate words and phrases for newsletters?
✔ Did I use interesting and appealing expressions regarding the topic?

Practice 1

Judge whether the meanings of the following sentences are T(true) or F(false).

1. '*Co.*' is an abbreviation for 'Corporation.' ( )
2. 'MBA' is a abbreviation for 'Master of Business Administration.' ( )
3. Organizing a newsletter begins by considering the readers of your writing. ( )

Writing Drills

The number one advantage of a newsletter is that it is a cost-effective means of communication, that is, a relatively inexpensive, but often very effective bulletin. Furthermore, this short written report contains news of interest chiefly to a special group, such as the recent activities of an organization and its members. Common topics covered in newsletters include business, products, jobs, energy, health, safety, and travel.

Newsletters can be divided into several sections depending on their purpose and readers. In this unit, you will learn and practice writing about school-related newsletters and business-related newsletters.

Part A. School-related Newsletters

In part A, you will learn and practice writing about school-related newsletters such as clubs, festivals, and employment. Bear in mind, it is important that you use appropriate words as well as appealing expressions and phrases on the topic to keep your readers interested.

Writing Model

Article No.: 100518854 Global Job Fair 2017 held at HUFS Global Campus

The Career Support Center of HUFS Global Campus hosted the Global Job Fair 2017 from November 1 to 2, 2017 at the Conference Hall, in the Centennial Complex.

Amid the recent rollout of 'blind hiring' and the increasing preference for practical experience among recruiters, the event was held under the subtitle of 'Resolving Job Seeking Troubles with Industry Experts.' It was attended by some 80 companies and recruiting agencies. They included Samsung Electronics, LG Electronics, SK Telecom, Amore Pacific, Coreana Cosmetics, NEXON Korea, Jusung Engineering, Yongin Job Center, and the Gyeonggi Provincial Foreign Investment Support Center.

The event was held with an industrial zone and a consulting zone. The industrial zone was divided into several sections: Finance/Sales/Marketing, Aerospace/Distribution/Trade, Science/Engineering, Management and Business Administration, and Public-Sector Corporations. During the Job Fair, students were given an opportunity to receive one-to-one consulting from those currently working at their dream company or industry. This personalized consulting was designed to help them build their capacity for their future career. In addition, the Job Fair offered a makeup clinic, a Tarot reading, and a photo booth for college job-seekers.

Questions about the Model

1. Where was the Job Fair held?

2. For whom did the make-up clinic serve?

Useful Expressions

Write other useful expressions fitting the titles.

A. Curriculum: all the courses of study offered by an educational institution

- required/essential subject vs. elective/optional course
- majors vs. minors vs. liberal arts
- extra-curricular activity
- distance learning (= remote learning) [lifelong education]
-
-

B. Examination: a formal test of a person's knowledge or proficiency in a particular subject, or to obtain a qualification.

- take an examination [pass an exam, fail an exam]
- an imminent examination [cram for an examination]
- re-take the course
- absolute evaluation vs. relative evaluation (= grade on a curve)
-
-

C. Semester: a half-year term in a school or university (typically lasting for fifteen to eighteen weeks, especially in North America)

- enter a school [graduate from a school, drop out of a school]
- start a new term
- I am so busy doing my homework.
- What will you do this vacation?
-
-

Brainstorming

Practice writing an article for a school newsletter with reference to one of the following topics.

- ✔ Introducing an event from your department
- ✔ Providing information about studying abroad as an exchange student
- ✔ Explaining to freshman students what to expect in their first year of study

Draft

Title:

Peer feedback

Part B. Business-related Newsletters

In part B, you will learn and practice writing about business-related newsletters such as recruitment, products, and public relations. Companies often issue newsletters for internal communication with employees and for promotion of their products, whereas nonprofit organizations issue them for their members.

Writing Model

KTO News

Title	[Korea] Korea Sale FESTA to Take Place in September

Photo: Korea Sale FESTA logo (Credit: Korea Sale FESTA)

This year's Korea Sale FESTA, a countrywide shopping event, is planned to take place from September 28 to October 7. Despite the shorter event period compared to previous years, the festival is expected to be greater than ever before. An opening concert featuring popular K-pop artists will be held at Seoul Plaza on September 27 in celebration of the event.

Event booths will be installed prior to and throughout the event period at Myeong-dong, Gangnam, Samseong Station and other major attraction areas within Seoul. Participating department stores as well as traditional markets will provide special offers. Traditional markets will also prepare special activity programs where visitors can experience Korea's traditional culture, pottery, regional cooking, and much more. Visitors can look forward to taking advantage of several convenient benefits during the festival period, such as receiving up to a 60% discount at major tourist attractions and accommodations as well as expanded services with the Korea Tour Card.

More Info: Korea Sale FESTA to Take Place in September

- ☞ Period: September 28 - October 7, 2018
- ☞ Location: Major cities including Seoul and its metropolitan area
- ☞ Korea Sale Festa website: www.koreasalefesta.kr (Korean, English, Japanese, Chinese)
- ☞ 1330 Korea Travel Hotline: +82-2-1330 (Korean, English, Japanese, Chinese, Russian, Vietnamese, Thai, Malay)

Questions about the Model

1. What is being promoted in the article?

....

2. Where would visitors be able to experience special activity programs like Korea's traditional culture?

....

Useful Expressions

Write other useful expressions fitting the titles.

A. Consumption: the act of buying and using things

- consumer protection
- deposit/withdraw/remit money in a bank
- lower class vs. middle class vs. upper class
-
-

B. Economy: the system (or financial condition) of a region or country in terms of the production and consumption of goods and services

- stabilize the economy vs. vitalize the economy
- developed countries (= advanced countries) vs. developing countries
- abolish regulations vs. loosen regulations vs. tighten up regulations
-
-

C. Production: the action of making or growing something in large quantities

- raise the price
- productivity enhancement
- increase price competitiveness
-
-

D. Labor: the human activity, especially hard physical work, that provides the goods or services in an economy

- negotiation between labor and management
- organize a labor union vs. join the trade union
- hire a worker vs. retain a worker vs. dismiss a worker
-
-

Brainstorming

Write an article contributing to a newsletter of a company or NGO with reference to one of the following topics.

- ✔ Promoting a new product of a corporation
- ✔ Describing the benefits of a new health food alternative
- ✔ Outlining the company's policies regarding dress codes

Draft

Title:

Peer feedback

Writing Tips

A. Writing Skills: Concord and Agreement

- **Concord:** There are some rules of grammatical concord that you must follow in English sentences.
  a. **[Tense]** I was hoping you would agree.
  b. **[Gender]** Whenever in trouble, she talks to herself.
  c. **[Number]** The headquarters of the United Nations is in New York.
  d. **[Case]** Our native professor is competent and warm-hearted, so everyone likes him.

- **Agreement:** The subject and verb of a sentence must agree on number, singular or plural, which is called the subject-verb agreement.
  (1) Agreement depends mainly on the head of the subject, or the noun phrase, but correlative conjunction sentences depend on the principle of proximity.
    a. The students in this classroom expect a good mark on the test.
    b. The number of attendees is thirty.
    c. A number of students are wearing glasses.
    d. Either you or I am to blame.

  (2) The singular is an "unmarked" number.
    a. Nobody knows. = Anybody does not know. = All people do not know.
    b. That we live without love is nonsense.

  (3) The number of 'part' or 'fraction' expressions depends on the following noun phrase.
    a. Some of the book is interesting.
    b. Some of the books are interesting.

  cf. *Every* and *each* are considered as singular.
    a. Every student has a talent for writing.
    b. Each of the nine members performs solo acts as well.

Practice 2 Complete the following sentences by selecting the most suitable words.

1. I as well as you (am / are) hungry.
2. The man who is holding papers in his hands (is / are) coming.
3. The rest of the questions (was / were) hard problems to solve.

B. Grammar Skills: Using the Passive

Every sentence must make a choice whether or not to use the active or passive voice. Of course, the active voice is the norm. However, the passive voice, which focuses on the object of the active form, is preferred for a few reasons as listed below. Passive sentences are usually used without a by-phrase being used as an agent.

(1) The agent is not known or not important.

a. I had my wallet stolen in the subway.

b. My grandfather was wounded in Korean civil war.

c. Rice is grown in Korea.

(2) The agent is obvious or refers to the general public.

a. I was invited to Rosa's party. (by Rosa)

b. Australia is also called Oz. (by people)

c. The criminal was arrested at Incheon International Airport. (by the police)

(3) You want to emphasize the topic, to avoid identifying the agent, or to avoid repeating of the agent especially in scientific and technical writing.

a. My project proposal has not yet been answered.

b. The shocking news story was leaked to the press over the weekend.

d. The subject was blindfolded and a pen was placed in the right hand.

• *Get* passive: Get means the idea of change; beginning or growing to be.

a. Mr. Hong got fired.

b. They are getting married next week.

c. You have to get accustomed to an 'early to bed and early to rise' routine.

Practice 3 Practice writing passive sentences by using the given words.

1. (movie, play)

▷ ....

2. (information, remove)

▷ ....

3. (get)

▷ ....

C. Collocation Drills by Subjects

Select one of the words in parenthesis to complete the sentence.

(1) School-related newsletters

- Which club do you want to (join / serve)?
- The (literacy / literary) rate of Korea has risen to 99%
- I'm worried that I have to (cram / crave) for the finals.
- I was very busy (doing / to do) all my vacation homework yesterday.
- I'm considering (double / twice) majoring in computer science and statistics.
- The subject, Academic English, is a (requested / required) course for graduation.
- TOEIC represents Test of English for International (Company / Communication), and FLEX stands for Foreign Language EXamination.
- SAT stands for Scholastic (Aptitude / Attitude) Test, TOEFL stands for Test of English as a Foreign Language, and GRE stands for Graduate Record Examination.

(2) Business-related newsletters

- The rich (go / get) richer and the poor (go / get) poorer.
- He (found / withdrew) the money that had been deposited for 10 years.
- The labor union (neglect / negotiated) a wage increase with the management.
- What's the (exchange / expected) rate for the Korean won to the U.S. dollar?
- The Korea Consumer Agency has worked for consumer (conservation / protection).
- The government announced its plan to (rise / raise) the price of diesel fuel to cut back fine dust emissions.
- Our company has experienced drastic corporate (constructing / restructuring) because of the financial crisis.
- The government should (abolish / trigger) laws and regulations undermining market competition across business sectors to enhance worker efficiency.

Writing Assignments 3

Write a contribution to a school newsletter based on your draft in Writing Drills Part A.

Brainstorming

Outline

Final

Title:

Writing Templates 3

{N: noun (phrase), to-V: to infinitive, S: subject, V: verb, that ~: that clause}

A. Agreement

- I (completely[partly]) agree with[to/about/on] N.
- I assent to[approve of] N.
- I agree with the opinion[point] that ~.
- I can see no reason to oppose ~.

e.g.

a. Basically, I agree with what you said.

b. The policy is perfectly clear and I can see no reason to oppose it.

c.

d.

B. Opposition

- I don't think that ~.
- I object to N[that ~].
- I (completely[partly]) disagree[don't agree] with N.
- I am against[opposed to] N.
- I disapprove of N[the fact that ~].
- I don't accept[believe/acknowledge/recognize/concede] that ~

e.g.

a. Nevertheless, I entirely disagree with that view.

b.

c.

C. Explanation

- In other words[That is (to say)], S + V.
- To put it another way, S + V.
- (To put it) concretely, S + V.
- In the strict sense (of the word), S + V.

e.g.

a. In other words, each color affects our mind.

b.

c.

D. Example

- For example[For instance], S + V.
- An example of N is ~.
- I'll take the example of N.
- Let's say, S + V.
- Let's take the example[case] of N.

e.g.

a. Let's say, I'm not quite sure about the topic.

b.

c.

E. Reason

- There are several[three] (main) reasons for[causes of] N.
- There are several[three] (main) reasons that ~[why ~].
- Because[As/Since/Now that] S + V, S + V.
- S + V, for S +V.
- For this[the above] reason, S + V
- The (main[basic/primary]) reason (for N) is that ~.
- This is (mainly) because S + V.

e.g.

a. I am not sure, but there may be several reasons for that.

b.

c.

F. Condition

- If S + V, S + V.
- In that S + V, S + V.
- In that[such a] case, S + V.
- Considering[In consideration of/In view of/In light of] N, S + V.
- Taking into account N[Taking N into consideration], S + V.

e.g.

a. He looks young considering his age.

b.

c.

Consumer Counseling | KCA News | Information | About KCA

KCA improves the Quality of People's lives
By adding Value and Trust in Consumer

We are witnessing rapid changes in the consumer enviroment thanks in part to globalization of the marketplace. and technological developmet which has enabled the CONSUMER market to expand from offline to online.

KCA News

KCA News
Korea Consumer Agency

Press Release

> KCA News > Press Release

Press Release

Total : 409 1/41 page

List 10 View

NO.	Title	Date	Count
409	Attention needs to be paid to incidents of children swallowing magnets NEW	2018-07-30	9
408	ICPEN's Call to Businesses In the Digital Economy	2018-07-26	19
407	More than half of the consumer disputes over clothing products occur due to business operator(s)'faults	2018-07-11	62
406	KCA distributed casebooks and manuals related to consumer damage arising from overseas direct purchases	2018-07-05	83

Unit 4

Travel Descriptions

Objectives

- To identify the basic format and contents of travel descriptions
- To learn the romanization of Korean and customary expressions related to travel
- To understand and practice the word order of noun phrases
- To understand and practice using commonly confused words

“Remember
that happiness is a way of travel - not a destination.”

– Roy M. Goodman

“A man
travels the world over
in search of what he needs
and returns home to find it.”

– George Moore

Warm-up Activity

Writing Model

Romantic Cherry Blossom Trip to Jinhae Gunhangje Festival

Gyeonghwa Station (Credit: Changwon-si)

Jinhae Gunhangje Festival is Korea's biggest spring festival, attracting at least 2 million visitors every year. The festival first began as a memorial service to commemorate Joseon period's most noteworthy naval admiral Yi Sun-sin and has now grown to become a festival enjoyed by everyone. Pack up and get ready to enjoy one of the most spectacular events in Korea surrounded by unbelievably stunning cherry blossoms!

Wonderful harmony of cherry blossoms and starlight, Yeojwacheon Starlight Festival

Yeojwacheon Starlight Festival (Credit: Changwon-si)

Yeojwacheon Starlight Festival is an evening event where Yeojwacheon Stream and Romance Bridge are decorated with illuminations and laser lights. This nighttime event is a must-visit festivity as the mesmerizing sight offers a different atmosphere from daytime.

Time travel to the Joseon Dynasty, Victory Parade

Victory Parade (Credit: Changwon-si)

The Victory Parade reenacts the victory march held by Admiral Yi Sun-sin and his army after winning a battle in the Imjin War (1592-1598). Viewers will be able to get a glimpse of Korea's history through the parade.

- **Period:** 15:00-16:00 April 6, 2018
- **Location:** Jungwon Rotary and city streets

What is a Travel Description?

A travel description is a written account of some useful information on travel. In addition to introducing tourist attractions, the contents of travel descriptions can include transportation, accommodations, performances, festivals, shopping, and food items.

When you write a travel description, there are several tips for you to consider. Before writing a draft, it is helpful for you to check the list below.

- Who your audience will be.
- Where you will be posting your writing.
- Whether or not to write your travel description based on your own experience.
- Whether or not to use the latest useful information available.
- Whether or not to use intriguing sightseeing photos.
- Which of the five W's and one H you will talk about in your description.
- Whether or not to offer contact numbers or website address so that the audience may obtain additional information.

Now, let's take a look at a sample and study the romanization rules of Korean.

Recommended Trails for a Walking Vacation on Jeju Island

[Photo: Seongsan Ilchulbong Peak along Route 1]

[Photo: Route 1-1 on U-do (island) Olle]

If you're looking for an eco-friendly vacation spot where you can enjoy the beautiful scenery while walking on a well-maintained trail to stay fit, there's no better place to go than Jeju Island. In the local dialect, "Olle" originally referred to the narrow path between the street and one's doorstep. Jeju Olle-gil, a series of walking trails that stretch around the entire coast of the island, is one of the many attractions and activities that Jeju has to offer. The trails pass through various landscapes along the way, including small villages, beaches, farms and forests. Each route offers a unique opportunity to soak in the beauty of Jeju and the island's culture.

There are currently a total of 26 routes that consist of 21 main routes and five sub-routes. The course differs in length and difficulty, allowing visitors to choose the appropriate course that meets each individual's level. The shortest route takes approximately one hour and the longest up to eight hours to complete. As each course is aided by direction signs and guiding posts along the way, even first-time visitors can conveniently find their way.

Romanization of Korean

(An excerpt from *The National Institute of the Korean Language*)

1. Basic Principles for Transcription
   (1) Romanization is based on standard Korean pronunciation.
   (2) No symbols except Roman letters are used so far as possible.

2. Summary of the Transcription System
   (1) Vowels are transcribed as follows:

• Simple Vowels

ㅏ	ㅓ	ㅗ	ㅜ	ㅡ	ㅣ	ㅐ	ㅔ	ㅚ	ㅟ
a	eo	o	u	eu	i	ae	e	oe	wi

• Diphthongs

ㅑ	ㅕ	ㅛ	ㅠ	ㅒ	ㅖ	ㅘ	ㅙ	ㅝ	ㅞ	ㅢ
ya	yeo	yo	yu	yae	ye	wa	wae	wo	we	ui

Note 1 : 'ㅢ' is transcribed as 'ui', although being pronounced as 'ㅣ'.

Note 2 : Long vowels are not reflected in transcription.

(2) Consonants are transcribed as follows:

• Plosives (Stops)

ㄱ	ㄲ	ㅋ	ㄷ	ㄸ	ㅌ	ㅂ	ㅃ	ㅍ
g, k	kk	k	d, t	tt	t	b, p	pp	p

• Affricates, Fricatives, Nasals, and Liquids

Affricates			Fricatives			Nasals			Liquids
ㅈ	ㅉ	ㅊ	ㅅ	ㅆ	ㅎ	ㄴ	ㅁ	ㅇ	ㄹ
j	jj	ch	s	ss	h	n	m	ng	r, l

Note 1 : The sounds ㄱ, ㄷ, and ㅂ are transcribed respectively as g, d, and b before a vowel; they are transcribed as k, t, and p when they appear before another consonant or as the last sound of a word. (They are transcribed as pronunciation in [ ].)

구미	Gumi	영동	Yeongdong	백암	Baegam
옥천	Okcheon	합덕	Hapdeok	호법	Hobeop
월곶[월곧]	Wolgot	벚꽃[벋꼳]	beotkkot	한밭[한받]	Hanbat

Note 2 : ㄹ is transcribed as r before a vowel, and as l before a consonant or at the end of a word: ㄹㄹ is transcribed as ll.

구리	Guri	설악	Seorak
칠곡	Chilgok	임실	Imsil
울릉	Ulleung	대관령[대괄령]	Daegwallyeong

Draft

You are contributing to a travel website. Write a travel description based on your experience.

Writing Checklist: Travel Description

As you write a travel description, review the checklist below and ask yourself the following questions.

- ✔ Did I check the basic formatting rules of writing travel descriptions?
- ✔ Did I use appropriate customary expressions in my travel descriptions?
- ✔ Did I give the necessary information needed based on the *five W's and one H*.

Practice 1

Judge whether the following sentences are T(true) or F(false).

1. Romanization is based on standard Korean pronunciation. (   )
2. 'ㅢ' is transcribed as 'ui', although being pronounced as 'ㅣ'. (   )
3. 'ㄹ' is transcribed as 'r' before a vowel, and as 'l' before a consonant or at the end of a word. (   )

Writing Drills

Part A. Domestic Travel Descriptions

In part A, you will learn about and practice writing domestic travel descriptions. For example, you may write about famous tourist attractions in Korea that you would like to introduce to your foreign friends. One of the most important considerations is whether or not your writing is based on your own experience.

Writing Model

[Photo: Insa-dong streets]

(Insa-dong: Jongno 3(sam)-ga Station, Exit 1, approx. 10-min walk)

One of Seoul's representative tourist attractions is none other than the traditional streets of Insa-dong. Many shops selling books, antiques and traditional products can be found here. Visitors can also experience the traditional art culture as traditional houses converted into art galleries and museums are available, as well as the popular art street, Ssamzie-gil Road. Another attraction not to be missed in Insa-dong is the variety of delicious foods being sold at traditional restaurants and by street vendors.

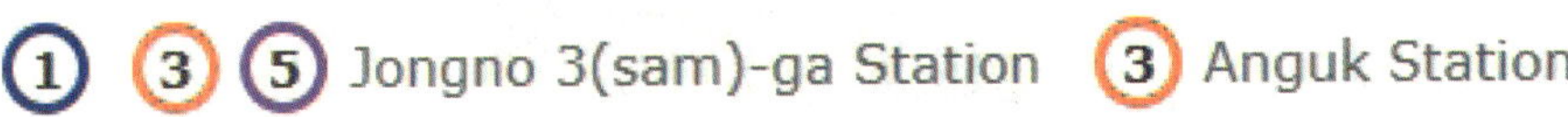

☞ Connecting Station: Jongno 3(sam)-ga Station (Seoul Subway Line 1, 3, 5) / Anguk Station (Seoul Subway Line 3)

Questions about the Model

1. Besides traditional restaurants, who are selling a variety of delicious foods at Insa-dong street?

2. What would you like to do in Insa-dong?

Useful Expressions

Write other useful expressions fitting the titles.

A. Stores

- a souvenir store vs. an antique store vs. a flea market
- a convenience store vs. a drugstore vs. a pharmacy
- a department store vs. a shopping mall vs. a grocery store
- ....
- ....

B. Antonyms

- peak time vs. off-peak time [busy season vs. off-season(slow season)]
- in season vs. out of season
- indoor sports vs. outdoor sports
- ....
- ....

C. Travel

- take a holiday trip
- Some day, I will take a tour of Jeju-do on foot.
- He is about to set off on a round-the-world backpacking trip.
- ....
- ....

Kimchi

Korea's Greatest Food

Kimchi is the most famous traditional food and icon that well-represents Korea itself, as it accompanies almost every meal served in the country. The name of the dish also differs depending on the main ingredient used, where cabbage, radish or cucumber most often play the main role. In addition, there are many variations in recipes and forms, offering the fun of tasting different textures and flavors from all across the nation. In addition, kimchi is gaining more attention nowadays worldwide due to its enormous nutritional value, becoming an international health food not just limited to Korea.

Brainstorming

Write a travel description with reference to one of the following topics.

- ✔ A Korean tourist attraction that you would like to introduce to your foreign friends
- ✔ A famous Korean dish (that originated in your home town)
- ✔ A location that is "off the beaten path" that most tourists don't know about but can be a good travel spot to meet locals

Draft

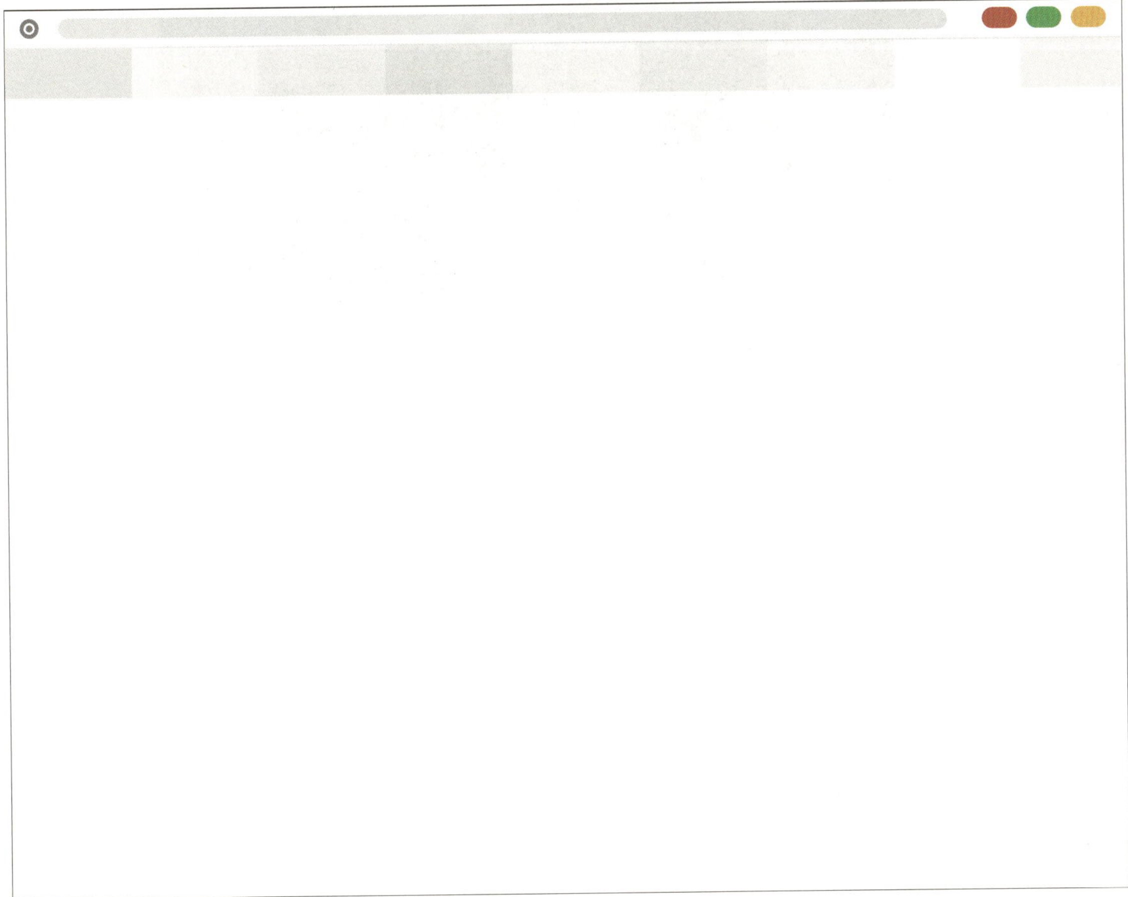

Peer feedback

Part B. Overseas Travel Descriptions

In part B, you will learn about and practice writing overseas travel descriptions. For example, you may write about famous tourist attractions in other countries that you would like to introduce to your Korean friends. The travel destinations that you talk about can be world famous attractions or about a place that you find most impressive.

Writing Model

Movie Studio Tours

Behind-the-scenes tours at Universal Studios' Hollywood lot

In 1915, Universal Studios Hollywood began the then-novel practice of giving the public a behind-the-scenes peek at its movie factory. Today, Universal has mostly morphed into a theme park with thrill rides and shows, but its classic Studio Tour tram still offers a fun overview of moviemaking. More focused on the details of film and TV production is the Warner Bros. Studio Tour. Aboard an oversized golf cart, you're whisked around the studio's facility in Burbank, visiting outdoor sets, a working soundstage and a museum packed with original movie props and costumes. Along the same line, the Paramount Pictures Studio Tour (near central Hollywood) and Sony Pictures Studio Tour (about 12 kilometers southwest of Hollywood in Culver City) offer small-group walking tours that explore their respective studio lots.

Questions about the Model

1. Of the movie studio tours, which one offers the small-group walking tours?

2. Which scenes would you especially want to see if you tour the movie studios?

Useful Expressions

Write other useful expressions fitting the titles.

A. Film ratings [Am.]

- G : general audience
- PG : parental guidance
- PG-13 : parental guidance suggested for children under thirteen
- R : restricted
- NC-17 or X : not for children under seventeen

B. Trip abroad

- a duty-free shop
- VWP(Visa Waiver Program) vs. a passport
- GMT(Greenwich Mean Time) vs. local time
- an embassy [an ambassador] vs. a consulate [a consul]
- check-in vs. boarding pass vs. boarding time

C. Travel

- I often enjoy exotic experiences.
- I'd like to broaden my horizons through travel.
- Someday, I will traverse the European continent.
- We traveled coast-to-coast by car during the last vacation.

Brainstorming

Write a travel description with reference to one of the following topics.

- ✔ An overseas tourist attraction that you would like to introduce to your classmates
- ✔ A popular backpacking route in Europe
- ✔ A location that you believe everyone should visit within their lifetime

Draft

Peer feedback

Writing Tips

A. Writing Skills: The Word Order of Noun Phrase

- **Noun Phrase (NP):** An element being used as a subject, object, and complement is not a noun but a noun phrase. A count noun itself is not used as a noun phrase unlike other nouns, such as pronouns, proper nouns, and non-count nouns.

a. We cannot wish for what we don't know. (pronouns ⇨ NP)
b. Every Jack has his Jill. (proper nouns ⇨ NP)
c. The sea complains it wants water. (non-count nouns ⇨ NP)

d. *Don't judge *book* by its cover. (count nouns)
e. Don't judge a book by its cover. (determiners + count nouns ⇨ NP)
f. Parents cannot never teach the use of books. (count nouns + -(e)s ⇨ NP)

- **The Word Order of NP:** Every NP has a strict word order. The premodification structure of NP is as follows.

NP: Pre-det.	+	Det.	+	Post-det. (ordinal + quantifier)		+	Adj.	+	Noun
e.g. *all*		*the*		*second*	*two*		*tall*		*boys*

· Pre-determiners: multipliers and fractions (*all, both, half, double, twice, ...*)
· Determiners: articles, possessives, demonstratives, and indefinite adjectives
(*the, my, some, any, no, each, either, ...*)
· Ordinals: *first, second, next, last, other, another, ...*
· Quantifiers: *one, two, many, much, few, little, ...*

a. Both (the) young men were successful.
b. The two young men were successful.
c. Both of the young men were successful.
d. The second World War (= World War 2)

Practice 2 Judge the grammaticality of the underlined words in the following sentences by writing T(true) or F(false).

1. We elected him president. The president is my uncle. (　　)
2. The professor collected our homework. (　　)
3. The professor hasn't returned our assignment yet. (　　)

B. Grammar Skills : Commonly Confused Words (1)

(1) **already** vs. **still** vs. **yet**

a. Have you already met Professor Lee? [I think you've probably met him.]

b. Have you met Professor Lee yet? [I don't know whether you've met him.]

c. I still can't speak English well, after all my years of study.

d. I can't speak English well yet, but I hope I will be able to soon.

(2) **also** vs. **as well** vs. **too**

a. Yeji not only sang; she also danced.

b. Yeji not only sang; she danced as well.

c. Yeji not only sang; she danced too.

(3) **farther** vs. **further**

a. Busan is farther than Gwangju from Seoul. ['be far (from)']

b. For further information, refer to the dictionary. ['additional', or 'more advanced']

cf. In sentence a., 'further' is possible.

(4) **affect** vs. **effect**

a. Stress affects my health in a negative way.

b. Stress has a negative effect on my health.

(5) **by** vs. **until** vs. **to**

a. You have to submit your term paper by next class.

b. Can I keep my baggage here with you until 3:00?

c. Our office hours are from 9:30 to 5:30.

Practice 3 Complete the following sentences by selecting the most suitable words.

1. By the way, I haven't eaten lunch (already / still / yet).
2. Sports can (also / as well / too) deliver the addictive qualities of a drug.

3. Colors (affect / effect) our feelings as well.
4. He sometimes drives from the office (by / until / to) the cafeteria.
5.~6. Once in Asia, genetic evidence suggests, the population split. One group stalled temporarily in the Middle East, while the other commenced a journey which would last tens of thousands of years. Moving a little (farther / further) with each new generation, they followed the coast around the Arabian Peninsula, India, and Southeast Asia, all the way to Australia. "The movement was probably imperceptible," says Spencer Wells. "It was less of a journey and probably more like walking a little (farther / further) down the beach to get away from the crowd." (Reading Explorer 4. p83.)

C. Collocation Drills by Subjects

Select one of the words in parenthesis to complete the sentence.

(1) Domestic Travel Descriptions

- Fruits (in / on) season are tasty and good for the body.
- The hotels are always full during the (peak / low) season.
- There is a (convenient / convenience) store at the corner.
- Someday, I'd love to go on a (all / round)-the-world cruise.
- This fan with oriental art on it is a nice (source / souvenir) from Korea.
- Call the front desk if you need a (morning / wake-up) call.
- I'd like to (make / take) a reservation for dinner tonight.
- If you don't want housekeeping services, hang up the ("Do Not Disturb" / "Don't Worry") sign.

(2) Overseas Travel Descriptions

- Through travel, we can (broaden / deepen) our horizons!
- When is the (check-in / boarding pass / boarding time)?
- Where is international (check-in / boarding pass / boarding time)?
- May I see your passport and (check-in / boarding pass / boarding time)?
- A duty-(free / off) shop is available in the International Terminal.
- (NC-17 / PG) says under no circumstances can you bring a child.
- We shall be landing shortly. Please fasten your (buttons / seatbelts).
- Renting a car in another country may require an international driver's (insurance / license).

Writing Assignments 4

Write a travel description based on one of your previous two drafts in Writing Drills Part A and B.

Brainstorming

Outline

Final

Writing Templates 4

{N: noun (phrase), to-V: to infinitive, S: subject, V: verb, that ~: that clause}

A. Comparison

- There are several[three] similarities[differences] between A and B.
- A and B are similar[different] in many[some] ways.
- A is similar to[different from] B in several[three] ways.
- A is similar to[different from] B in (the fact) that ~.
- The (main[basic/primary]) similarities[differences] between A and B are that ~.
- Relatively[Comparatively], S + V.
- Compared[In comparison] with[to] N, S + V.
- Like this[In this way/In this manner], S + V.
- Similarly[Likewise/In similar fashion/In like manner/In the same way], S + V

e.g.

a. There are several similarities between the two travels.

b.

c.

B. Contrast

- In[By] contrast, S + V
- Contrarily[Conversely/On the contrary], S + V
- In contrast to N, S + V
- Unlike this, S + V.
- On the one hand ~, on the other (hand) ~.
- S + V ~, while[whereas] S + V.

e.g.

a. In contrast, the average weight decreased for all groups.

b.

c.

C. Concession

- Despite[In spite of] N[the fact that ~], S + V.
- Though[Although/Even if/Even though] S + V, S + V.
- However[Nevertheless/Nonetheless], S + V.
- Anyway[Anyhow/In any case/In any event/At any rate], S + V.

e.g.

a. Despite all the evidence, I don't want to believe it.

b. ....

....

c. ....

....

D. Comparative

- A is (even[still/much/(by) far/a lot]) more ~ than B.
- The more ~, the more ~.
- S + V~ all the better for N.
- S + V the more ~ of the two N.
- A is no more B than C is D. = A is not B any more than C is D.

e.g.

a. The sooner (you did it), the better (it will be).

b. I like you all the better for your faults.

c. Of the two suggestions, the former seems much more reasonable.

d. A whale is no more a fish than a horse is.

e. ....

....

f. ....

....

E. Superlative

- S is the most ~ in Nsg.[of all (the) Npl.]. {Nsg.: singular noun, Npl.: plural noun}

e.g.

a. John is the tallest in our class[of all our classmates].

= John is as tall as any student in his class.

= No (other) student in the class is as tall as[taller than] John.

= Tom is taller than any other student[all the other students/anyone else] in his class.

b.

c.

cf.

- no more than + 'numeral' = only ~ OR as few[little] as ~
- no less than + 'numeral' = as many[much] as ~
- not more than + 'numeral' = at most ~
- not less than + 'numeral' = at least ~

e.g.

a. I have no more than ten dollars. = I have only ten dollars.

b.

c.

d.

florence
siena
travel ITALY
venice

Unit 5

Resumes and Cover Letters

Objectives

- To identify the basic format and contents of a resume and a cover letter
- To learn the customary words and expressions in a resume and cover letter
- To understand and practice using quantifiers
- To understand and practice using commonly confused words

“The future belongs to
those who prepare for it today.”

– Malcolm X

“A dream
doesn't become reality through magic;
it takes sweat, determination and hard work.”

– Colin Powell

Warm-up Activity

Writing Model

Ho Jung Yu
1700 S College Ave #28, Tempe, AZ 85281
480-326-8536 ho.yu@asu.edu

October 30, 2008

Arizona State University
AECP Screening Committee 1
Box 873504
Tempe, AZ 85287-3504

Dear AECP Screening Committee:

I am eager to pursue a teaching position in AECP at Arizona State University after completing my Ph.D. in Rhetoric/Composition & Linguistics in December, 2008.

I have taught learners who have many different levels of English and ethnic backgrounds. Most recently, I have been teaching various English composition courses in diverse classroom contexts at ASU for four and a-half years as a teaching associate. This position has helped me to develop as a practitioner and researcher. Throughout my time teaching, I have conducted IRB classroom-based research studies to cultivate pedagogical practices and theories accumulated via graduate studies, participated in workshops, and observed other teachers, as well as myself. I have presented the findings of my research studies at several national and international conferences, such as *Symposium on Second Language Writing, IAWE (The International Association of World Englishes) International Conference: International Conference on Globalization and World), and Asia TEFL International Conference* to name a few. These efforts continue to assist me to better understand students' personal or academic needs, especially at ASU. Therefore, I can help students connect their learning to their individual goals and contexts that they are involved in. I believe that my learning experience, teaching experience, and multicultural competences will best serve students at AECP. Additionally, I would like to support AECP by promoting this prestigious program in South Korea.

I hope that my interest and abilities meet the expectations of AECP. I appreciate your taking the time to review my resume and other materials. I look forward to your reply.

Respectfully yours

Ho Jung Yu

What are a Resume and a Cover Letter?

A résumé is a summary of your personal background and your qualifications. A resume is to employment what a passport is to travel. A well-organized structured and well-written resume helps potential employers see at a glance whether you are suited for a job opening or not. There are two types of resumes. One is a chronological resume for someone just out of college, and the other is a functional resume for a more experienced person.

Along with your resume, the cover letter — also a covering letter or note — aims to introduce yourself briefly and to make an employer interested in you. You should include only the high points of your information in your resume.

Now, let's identify the basic format and useful expressions of a resume and a cover letter.

Basic format of a cover letter

① Head: - NAME
- Address, City, Country, Zip Code,
- Mobile Number,
- E-mail Address

② Date

③ Inside Address: - Contact Person's Name and Title
- Company Name and Address

④ Subject: Title of Position being applied for

⑤ Salutation

⑥ Body:
- ■ Purpose or Reason for Writing
- ■ Related Core Skills or Qualification

⑦ Closing

⑧ Name or Signature

※ If necessary, inform about enclosed materials

Basic format of a resume

NAME

(Contact Information)
- Address
- Mobile Number
- E-mail Address

Objective

(Qualifications Summary)

Experience

Skills

Education
(Major Courses)
(Related Courses)
(Special School Project)

(Work)
(Volunteer Activities)

Certifications

(Awards or Honors)

References

Synonyms and antonyms related to personality

	Positive	Negative
1	outgoing, extrovert(ed)	introspective, introvert(ed), reserved, withdrawn
2	progressive, go-ahead	conservative, inflexible
3	active, aggressive, assertive, affirmative, positive, optimistic	passive, negative, pessimistic
4	open-minded	narrow-minded
5	caring, altruistic, selfless	egocentric, selfish
6	good-natured	hard to please, picky
7	sociable, cooperative	nonsociable, noncooperative

Draft

Write your resume in the way of chronological, functional, or combined order.

Writing Checklist: Resumes and Cover Letters

As you write your resume or cover letters, review the checklist below and ask yourself the following questions.

- ✔ Did I obey the basic formatting rules of resumes and cover letters?
- ✔ Did I comply with the customary expressions of resumes and cover letters?
- ✔ Did I try to call attention to my best features and downplay my disadvantages without misrepresenting or distorting?

Practice 1

Judge whether the meanings of the following expressions are T(true) or F(false).

1. The word, altruistic, is the antonym of the word, egocentric. ( )
2. In a resume, the contact information is optional. ( )

Writing Drills

Part A. Resumes

In part A, you will learn about and practice writing a resume. Especially, your resume should be clear and easy on the eyes as employers may not spend much time reading it.

Writing Model

Hailey Lee

E-mail: haileylee1234@gmail.com
Phone: +82) 10-8888-8888
Linkedin Profile: www.linkedin.com/in/hailey-lee-a86402500
Address: 123, Baegok-daero 2402beon-gil, Mohyeon-eup,
Cheoin-gu, Yongin, Gyeonggi-do, South Korea, Zip Code 12345

Objective

The position of Accounting Associate

Qualifications Summary

- +1 year internship in a law office in California, USA
- Knowledge of general accounting principles/procedures
- Intermediate level of proficiency with Microsoft Office Suite
- Strong communication skills; trilingual in English, Korean and Chinese

Education

1. **Hankuk University of Foreign Studies (HUFS),** Yong-in, South Korea
   - Field of Study: Double major in International Business and Chinese Translation & Interpretation
   - Type of Degree: Bachelor's Degree
   - Institution Start Date: March 01, 2012 ~ Expected Graduation Date: August 17, 2018
   - Relevant Coursework: *Accounting Principal, Theory of International Financial Management, Introduction to Economics, Principles of Accounting, International Management Strategy*

2. **ABC Academy** (AICPA), Seoul, South Korea
   - Institution Start Date: July, 2016~ End Date: November, 2016
   - Relevant Coursework (Total 240 hours):
   - *Accounting Principal, Intermediate Accounting I, Intermediate Accounting II, Managerial Accounting, Taxation I, Taxation II, Business Law, Auditing and Attestation I*

Work Experience

1. Law Offices of HUFS, San Francisco, California, U.S.A.
   - Position: Immigration Department Intern
   - From November, 2016 to October, 2017 (Total 12 months)

Tasks/ Responsibilities:

· Keep cases organized; meeting deadlines; inputting information into file database and case management software; confirming case status with attorney; Translate Korean and Chinese documents into English
· Keep clients informed by maintaining contact, communicating case progress

Education Abroad

- Mandarin Training Center, National Taiwan Normal University, National Sun Yat-sen University, Taiwan
  From March, 2014 to February, 2015 (Total 12 months)

Skills & Certifications

- Language Skills: English-Intermediate / Korean-Native / Chinese–Intermediate
- MS Office Skills: Word-Advanced / Excel-Advanced / PowerPoint-Advanced
- Special Awards/Honors/Certifications:
· Tuition assistance awarded for the second semester of 2013 (for working as a student journalist)
· Scholarship awarded for the second semester of 2012

(Volunteer Activities)

1. Immigrant Worker Center, Yong-in, South Korea, From August, 2013 to December, 2013, Korean Teacher
2. Community Children Center, Yong-in, South Korea, From March, 2012 to June, 2012, Teacher & Counselor

Useful Expressions

Write other useful expressions in relation to the title, a resume.

- Reference available upon request (= Provided upon request)
- Fluency in English and Chinese [spoken & written]
- Able to address clients' diverse needs
- A challenging position in the computer technology field
- Majored in Statistics with a minor in Business Administration
- Expected to graduate from Hankuk University of Foreign Studies in February 2024
- ....
- ....

Brainstorming

Suppose you are applying for an internship program of a company or NGO. Compose a handwritten resume for your application.

Draft

Peer feedback

Part B. Cover Letters

In part B, you will learn about and practice writing a cover letter. Keep in mind, it is especially important to emphasize why you are the best candidate for the job.

Writing Model

Eileen Shim

81, Oedae-ro, Mohyeon-eup,
Cheoin-gu, Yongin-si, Gyeonggi-do, Republic of Korea
Phone: +82-10-1234-5678, E-mail: eileen.shim@email.com

March 21, 2018

Mr. Olaf Eriksson, Principal
Danderyds Gymnasium
36b Rinnig Nasa Gatan,
18773 Taby, Sweden

Dear Mr. Eriksson,

I am interested in the internship position as an English teacher which you are offering at the moment. I am currently a student at Hankuk University of Foreign Studies majoring in English for Interpretation and Translation. I will graduate in one year, however my last 8 months in the school can be finished abroad, participating in an internship program.

I consider myself fluent in English and Swedish, and I would like the opportunity not only for my teaching practice, but to live in Sweden to test and improve my language proficiency. Also, for some time, I have hoped to go to Sweden since I heard that it is a beautiful country with interesting people. In the future, I would like to teach English to Swedish people and learn the culture. Therefore, this internship would be a great opportunity for me.

I am looking forward to your reply as soon as possible.

Sincerely yours,

Eileen Shim

Questions about the Model

1. What is the major of the applicant?

2. What do you think is the most important point in writing a cover letter?

Useful Expressions

Write other useful expressions fitting the titles.

A. Salutation & Introduction

- To whom it may concern
- I'm writing in response to your advertisement for a sales clerk.
- I'm writing to apply for the secretary position advertised on your website.
- ……………………………………
- ……………………………………

B. Body

- The opportunity to grow with your organization would be unparalleled
- I have a keen interest in establishing my career in the field of advertising.
- Since I majored in Business Administration, it has been my goal to work for your company.
- ……………………………………
- ……………………………………

C. Closing

- I will be available for an interview any time at your convenience.
- I look forward to hearing from you soon.
- Respectfully yours
- ……………………………………
- ……………………………………

Brainstorming

Suppose you are applying for an internship program of a company or NGO. Write a cover letter to be submitted along with your resume that you wrote in Part A.

Draft

Peer feedback

Writing Tips

A. Writing Skills: Using Quantifiers

- **Quantifiers:** A quantifier is a word or phrase that precede a (pro)noun, and indicates the number or amount of the (pro)noun. You can use quantifiers to refer to a quantity of something without being precise.

Number	Number/Amount	Amount
one/two/three/... many/many a a good[great] many a (large) number of few/a few several/a couple of	plenty of a lot of/lots of	much a (good/great) deal of a(a) (large) amount of little/a little

a. He who begins many things, finishes but few.
b. Many a person read his novel. (= Many people read his novel.)
c. How much time do you spend sending chat messages each day?

- **The Countability of Quantifiers (and Determiners):** A quantifier of number precedes a count noun, whereas a quantifier of amount precedes a noncount noun.
  cf. *All, most, some, a lot of*, and *plenty of* are all used with both plural count nouns and noncount nouns.

a. Nowadays, very few students learn Latin.
b. Don't worry, winter vacation will begin in a few days.
c. There are quite a few barriers to keep you from doing it.
d. A little knowledge is dangerous.
e. I have to devote a good deal of attention to the final exam.

f. Don't put all your eggs in one basket.
g. That's all water under the bridge now.

Practice 2 Judge the grammaticality of the underlined words in the following sentences by writing T(true) or F(false).

1. Empty vessels make the most sound. (   )
2. Most people realize only a small part of their potential. (   )
3. Most merchandise of the brand is known for high-quality products. (   )

B. Grammar Skills : Commonly Confused Words (2)

(1) **during** vs. **for**

a. What will you do during the winter *vacation*? [when something happens]

b. I'll take part in the Intensive English Program for *ten* days. [how long it lasts]

c. We all had a ball during *the* three days.

d. The tropical night phenomenon continued for *three* days.

(2) **although** vs. **though**

a. He was delighted at heart, although/though he spoke to the contrary.

b. Even although(X)/though he didn't understand a word, he kept smiling.

c. It was a quiet party, I had a good time, though/although(X).

(3) **high** vs. **tall**

a. Seo Jang-hoon is a very high(X)/tall man.

b. The high/tall building deprived their house of sunlight.

(4) **childlike** vs. **childish**

a. Ye-won never lost her childlike innocence, so she is very charming. [positive]

b. Isn't it time you grew out of such childish practices? [negative]

(5) **historic** vs. **historical**

a. The unification of the Korean Peninsula will be a very important historic event.

b. He is writing a historical novel about the mid-20th century Korean War.

Practice 3 Complete the following sentences by selecting the suitable words.

1. It rained (during / for) the night (during / for) three hours.
2. Chase after the truth like hell and you'll free yourself, even (although / though) you never touch its coat-tails. — *Clarence Darrow*
3. Who is the (highest/tallest) student in your our class?
4. Don't worry, I won't do anything (childlike / childish).
5. Despite his (historic / historical) feat, he lived a miserable life.

C. Collocation Drills by Subjects

Select one of the words in parenthesis to complete the sentence.

(1) Resume

- Reference available (to / upon) request
- (Accuracy / Fluency) in English and Spanish
- Graduated (from / with) honors
- Graduated (from / with) university
- (Scoring / Scored) 850 on the TOEIC
- BA (on / in) Business Administration
- (Proficient / Proficiency) in Excel, PowerPoint, and Web Graphic Design
- Visited UCLA for and as part of a student (change / exchange) program

(2) Cover Letter

- I am (enclosing / putting) my resume with this letter.
- I would like to (plan / schedule) an interview with you.
- I look forward to (debating / discussing) this position with you.
- I am interested in the secretary (job / position) at your company.
- A (challenging / challenged) position in the computer technology field.
- I believe that my experience and (quality / qualifications) make me perfect for this job.
- I would like to express my (intension / interest) in a possible job opening at your company.
- I'm a quick typist and very familiar (in / with) all the software programs such as Excel and PowerPoint.

Writing Assignments 5

Write a complete resume or cover letter developed from one of your two drafts in Writing Drills Part A and B.

Brainstorming

Outline

Final

Writing Templates 5

{N: noun (phrase), to-V: to infinitive, S: subject, V: verb, that ~: that clause}

A. Conclusion

- Finally[Eventually/Ultimately/After all/In the end/In the long run], S + V.
- In conclusion[To conclude], S + V.
- All in all, S + V ...
- My conclusion is that ~.
- I come to the conclusion that ~.
- For all these[he above-mentioned] reasons, S + V.
- In view of these facts, it is likely[probable] that ~.

e.g.

a. I came to the conclusion that love was everything at that time.

b.

c.

B. Result

- Therefore[So/Thus/Accordingly], S + V.
- Consequently[As a result/As a consequence], S + V.
- As a result[consequence] of N, S + V.
- With the result that ~, S + V.
- According to N[as S + V], S + V.
- The result[consequence] is that ~.

e.g.

a. As a consequence, it is necessary to review these books, TEOW1 and TEOW2 again and again.

b.

c.

C. Prospect

- In the (near) future, S + V.
- Soon[Shortly/Before long/Sooner or later], S + V.
- What this means[suggests/implies] is that ~.
- It is time (for us) to-V.

e.g.

a. In the near future, we will be able to get a drone taxi to avoid the rush hour traffic.

b. ....

c. ....

D. Summary

- To sum up, S + V.
- In summary[short/brief/sum/a word], S + V.
- To put it shortly[briefly], S + V.
- To make[cut] a long story short, S + V.

e.g.

a. To make a long story short, everything worked well.

b. ....

c. ....

E. Emphasis

- Especially[Particularly/In particular], S + V.
- Above all[First of all/Most of all/Among others/First and foremost], S + V.
- Mainly[Chiefly/Primarily/Principally], S + V.
- More importantly[significantly/particularly], S + V.
- To put it clearly[plainly], S + V.

e.g.

a. Above all things, learn to learn from past mistakes.

b.

c.

"Language is a mirror of the mind."

– Noam Chomsky

"The limits of my language are the limits of my world."

– Ludwig Josef Johann Wittgenstein

RESUME
RESUME
RESUME

Appendices

Appendix A. Connectors and Transitions
Appendix B. Abbreviations
Appendix C. Irregular Verbs

“What is written without effort
is in general read without pleasure.”

— Samuel Johnson.

Appendix A. Connectors and Transitions

Suitable connecting and/or transition words should be used in the proper places of your writing. It will help your ideas flow clearly. Connecting words [= Connectors] are coordinators(= coordinating conjunctions), correlative (paired) conjunctions, and subordinators(= subordinating conjunctions). Transition signals [= Transitions] are conjunctive adverbs, prepositions, and so on.
(cf. Refer to *Appendix A. Sentence Types and Connecting Words* of *THE ESSENCE OF WRITING 1.*)

a. My midterm scores are really terrible**, but** my final grades won't be that bad.
b. **Although** my midterm scores are really terrible**,** my final grades won't be that bad.
c. My midterm scores are really terrible**. However,** my final grades won't be that bad.
d. My midterm scores are really terrible**; however,** my final grades won't be that bad.

e. Ye-jun can speak **not only** English **but also** Chinese.
f. Ye-jun can speak Chinese **as well as** English.
g. Ye-jun can speak **both** English **and** Chinese.
h. **In addition to** speaking English, Ye-jun can speak Chinese.
i. **Besides** English, Ye-jun can speak Chinese.
j. Ye-jun can speak English, **and also** Chinese.
k. Ye-jun can speak English **and** Chinese, **too**.

	Coordinators [Correlative Conj.]	Subordinators	Transitions (Adv. & Prep.)
Addition	and both A and B not only A, but also B nor neither A nor B		also / besides / moreover / in addition / furthermore in addition to as well as too / also / as well
Alternative	or either A or B not A but B whether A or B	whether ~ whether or not ~ whether ~ or not if ~ (or not)	alternatively otherwise instead of

	Coordinators	Subordinators	Transitions (Adv. & Prep.)
Clarification			for example / for instance to illustrate in particular / (more) specially that is in other words more simply / in simpler words such as ~ like ~
Comparison (Similarities)			also similarly likewise in the same way (just) like
Conclusion			finally to sum up in summary / in conclusion to summarize / to conclude in brief / in short / in closing all in all as we have seen for these reasons
Condition		(even) if unless provided (that) in case when once as long as	
Contrast & Concession	but yet	although (even) though whereas while	however nevertheless nonetheless still in contrast on the one hand, ~ on the other hand, ~ conversely, instead (of) rather on the contrary even so admittedly unlike despite / in spite of

	Coordinators	Subordinators	Transitions (Adv. & Prep.)
Emphasis			actually in fact indeed
Frequency		as often as	
Manner		(just) as as if as though	
Place (Distance)		where wherever anywhere everywhere as far as as close as	
Purpose & Results	so	so that so ~ that such ~ that in order that	accordingly consequently as a result as a consequence therefore thus hence as a result of according to
Time & Order		after (just) as as long as as soon as before once until / till when whenever while since	first of all to begin with first and foremost first / second / third / ... next / later / afterward subsequently now soon then meanwhile / in the meantime after a while last (of all) finally / at last / after all above all / most of all
Reasons & Opinion	for	because since / as now that seeing that	because of due to owing to in my opinion[view]

Appendix B. Abbreviations

Abbreviations can save you time when you are writing informally or taking notes. However, you should use them with care in formal writing. Abbreviations are often used in e-mails, text messages, comments, news letters, travel descriptions, resumes and cover letters as well as various written forms. Frequently-used Latin abbreviations are as follows.

- cf. *(confer)* compare
- e.g. *(exampli gratia)* for example
- et al. *(et alii)* and others
- etc. *(et cetera)* and so on
- i.e. *(id est)* that is
- NB *(nota bene)* note well
- vs. *(vertere)* versus

Abbreviations are usually used for time, dates, titles, and initials in a person's name.

e.g. a. The class ended at 3:20 **p.m.**

b. The rice crop traces back to about 5000 **B.C.**

c. **Ms.** Parker / **Dr.** Lee / Martin Luther King **Jr.**

d. **W.** Shakespeare / Alfred **A.** Attanasio

Abbr.	Meaning	Abbr.	Meaning
sec.	second	Jan.	January
min.	minute	Feb.	February
hr.	hour	Mar.	March
a.m.	*(ante meridiem)* before noon	Apr.	April
p.m.	(post meridiem) after noon		May
Mon.	Monday	Jun.	June
Tue(s).	Tuesday	Jul.	July
Wed.	Wednesday	Aug.	August
Thur(s).	Thursday	Sept.	September
Fri.	Friday	Oct.	October
Sat.	Saturday	Nov.	November
Sun.	Sunday	Dec.	December
w/e	weekend	24/7	for twenty-four hours seven days a week

An abbreviation is a shortened form of a word or phrase, made by leaving out some of the letters or by using only the first letter of each word.

- **Acronyms:** Abbreviations formed from the initial letters of other words and pronounced as a word

e.g. a. *NASA* National Aeronautics and Space Administration
b. *UNICEF* United Nations Children's Fund
c. *radar* radio detecting and ranging

- **Initialisms(=Alphabetic Abbreviations):** Abbreviation formed from initial letters and pronounced separately

e.g. a. *BBC* British Broadcasting Corporation
b. *FBI* Federal Bureau of Investigation
c. *OECD* Organization for Economic Cooperation and Development

- **Clipping:** The deletion of some part of a longer word to give a shorter word with the same meaning

e.g. a. *ref~~erence~~* < ref. *prof~~essor~~* < *Prof.* *gym~~nasium~~* < *gym*
b. *~~tele~~phone* < *phone* *~~omni~~bus* < *bus* *~~cara~~van* < *van*

1. E-mail

- Re. Regarding
- Cc Carbon copy
- Bcc Blind carbon copy
- Attn Attention
- Rgds Regards
- ASAP As Soon As Possible
- RSVP please reply
- P.S. Post Script

2. Text Messages and Comments

- AFAIK as far as I know / and for all I know
- Approx. Approximately
- GA Go Ahead
- FWD forward
- CUL See You Later
- Pls Please

(cf. Refer to the Useful Chat Abbreviations of Unit 2. ☞ p. 37, 40)

3. News Letters

- CE — Common Era
  (cf. BC; Before Christ)
- BCE — Before the Common Era
  (cf. AD; *(Anno Domini)* in the year of the Lord)
- Dpt. — Department
- Univ. — University
- Asso(c). — Associate / Association

4. Travel Descriptions

- Ave. vs. St. — Avenue vs. Street
- ATM — Automated Teller Machine
- ATC — Air Traffic Control
- CIQ — Customs, Immigration and Quarantine
- DBC — Denied Boarding Compensation
- ETA — Estimated Time of Arrival
- ETD — Estimated Time of Departure
- FIT vs. GIT — Foreign Independent Tour vs. Group Inclusive Tour
- GMT — Greenwich Mean Time
- PNR — Passenger Name Record
- TIM — Travel Information Manual
- TWOV — transit without visa

5. Resumes and Cover Letters

- BA — Bachelor of Arts
- MA — Master of Arts
- MBA — Master of Business Administration
- CPA — Certified Public Accountant
- Encls. — Enclosures

(cf. Refer to other useful abbreviations of Unit 3. ☞ p. 57)

Appendix C. Irregular Verbs

Base form	Past	Past Participle
arise	arose	arisen
awake	awoke / awaked	awoken / awaked
be	was / were	been
bear	bore	borne
beat	beat	beaten
become	became	become
begin	began	begun
bend	bent	bent
bereave	bereft / bereaved	bereft / bereaved
beset	beset	beset
bet	bet / betted	bet / betted
bid	bid / bade	bid / bidden
bind	bound	bound
bite	bit	bitten
bleed	bled	bled
blow	blew	blown
break	broke	broken
breed	bred	bred
bring	brought	brought
broadcast	broadcast	broadcast
build	built	built
burn	burnt / burned	burnt / burned
burst	burst	burst
buy	bought	bought
cast	cast	cast
catch	caught	caught
choose	chose	chosen
cling	clung	clung
come	came	come
cost	cost	cost
creep	crept	crept
cut	cut	cut
deal	dealt	dealt
dig	dug	dug
dive	dived / *<AmE> dove*	dived
do	did	done
draw	drew	drawn
dream	dreamt / dreamed	dreamt / dreamed
drink	drank	drunk
drive	drove	driven
eat	ate	eaten
fall	fell	fallen
feed	fed	fed
feel	felt	felt
fight	fought	fought

Base form	Past	Past Participle
find	found	found
flee	fled	fled
fling	flung	flung
fly	flew	flown
forbid	forbad(e)	forbidden
forecast	forecast	forecast
forget	forgot	forgotten
forgive	forgave	forgiven
forsake	forsook	forsaken
freeze	froze	frozen
get	got	got / *<AmE> gotten*
give	gave	given
go	went	gone
grind	ground	ground
grow	grew	grown
hamstring	hamstrung	hamstrung
hang	hung	hung
cf. hang	*hanged*	*hanged*
have	had	had
hear	heard	heard
heave	hove / heaved	hove / heaved
hide	hid	hidden
hit	hit	hit
hold	held	held
hurt	hurt	hurt
keep	kept	kept
kneel	knelt / kneeled	knelt / kneeled
knit	knit / knitted	knit / knitted
know	knew	known
lead	led	led
lean	leant / leaned	leant / leaned
leap	leapt / leaped	leapt / leaped
learn	learnt / learned	learnt / learned
leave	left	left
lend	lent	lent
let	let	let
lie	lay	lain
cf. lie	*lied*	*lied*
lay	*laid*	*laid*
light	lit / lighted	lit / lighted
lose	lost	lost
make	made	made
mean	meant	meant
meet	met	met
mislead	misled	misled
misspell	misspelt / misspelled	misspelt / misspelled
mistake	mistook	mistaken
misunderstand	misunderstood	misunderstood

Base form	Past	Past Participle
mow	mowed	mown / mowed
offset	offset	offset
put	put	put
quit	quit / quitted	quit / quitted
read	read	read
rid	rid / ridded	rid / ridded
ride	rode	ridden
ring	rang	rung
cf. ring	*ringed*	*ringed*
rise	rose	risen
run	ran	run
saw	sawed	sawn / sawed
say	said	said
see	saw	seen
seek	sought	sought
sell	sold	sold
send	sent	sent
set	set	set
sew	sewed	sewn / sewed
shake	shook	shaken
shear	sheared	shorn / sheared
shed	shed	shed
shine	shone / shined	shone / shined
shoot	shot	shot
show	showed	shown
shrink	shrank	shrunk
shut	shut	shut
sing	sang	sung
sink	sank	sunk
sit	sat	sat
sleep	slept	slept
slide	slid	slid
sling	slung	slung
slit	slit	slit
smell	smelt / smelled	smelt / smelled
sow	sowed	sown / sowed
speak	spoke	spoken
speed	sped / speeded	sped / speeded
spell	spelt / spelled	spelt / spelled
spend	spent	spent
spill	spilt / spilled	spilt / spilled
spin	spun	spun
spit	spat / spit / spitted	spat / spit / spitted
split	split	split
spoil	spoilt / spoiled	spoilt / spoiled
spread	spread	spread
spring	sprang	sprung
stand	stood	stood

Base form	Past	Past Participle
steal	stole	stolen
stick	stuck	stuck
sting	stung	stung
stink	stank	stunk
stride	strode	stridden
strike	struck	struck
string	strung	strung
strive	strove / strived	striven / strived
swear	swore	sworn
sweat	sweat / sweated	sweat / sweated
sweep	swept	swept
swell	swelled	swollen / swelled
swim	swam	swum
swing	swung	swung
take	took	taken
teach	taught	taught
tear	tore	torn
telecast	telecast	telecast
tell	told	told
think	thought	thought
thrive	thrived	thrived
throw	threw	thrown
thrust	thrust	thrust
tread	trod	trodden
undergo	underwent	undergone
understand	understood	understood
undertake	undertook	undertaken
underwrite	underwrote	underwritten
uphold	upheld	upheld
upset	upset	upset
wake	woke / waked	woken / waked
wear	wore	worn
weave	wove	woven
wed	wed / wedded	wed / wedded
weep	wept	wept
wet	wet / wetted	wet / wetted
win	won	won
wind	wound	wound
withdraw	withdrew	withdrawn
withhold	withheld	withheld
withstand	withstood	withstood
wring	wrung	wrung
write	wrote	written

Answer Key

Answer Key

Unit 1 E-mail

Warm-up Activity; Practice 1, p. 18.

1. T 2. F 3. T

Writing Drills;

Part A: Questions about the Model, p. 20.

1. To tell him about an upcoming regular safety inspection
2. Be at his home

Part B: Questions about the Model, p. 22.

1. He wants to refund the overcharged delivery charge.
2. The word, DIY, means we make our own items by ourselves, as an abbreviation of 'do-it-yourself'.
3. The answer will vary.

Writing Tips;

B. Grammar Skills; Practice 3, p. 26.

1. F 2. N 3. N

C. Collocation Drills by Subjects, p. 27.

(1) earlier follow-up attached interest
career make cellular
make public forming

(2) revenue attaching comprehensive
calculate about replacement
neglect building workforce
prosperous

Unit 2 Text Messages and Comments

Warm-up Activity; Practice 1, p. 38.

1. T　　2. T

Writing Drills;

Part A: Questions about the Model, p. 40.

1. Douglas is going to be in charge of the catering.
2. They will use four cars.

Writing Tips;

A. Writing Skills; Practice 2, p. 45.

1. Moreover　　2. nevertheless　　3. In contrast

B. Grammar Skills; Practice 3, p. 46.

1. T　　2. T　　3. F

C. Collocation Drills by Subjects, p. 47.

(1) information	way	kidding
frequently	phone	other
regard	POV	on
try		
(2) up	so	come
wish	beyond	from
make	to accept	place
business		

Unit 3 News Letters

Warm-up Activity; Practice 1, p. 58.

1. F　　2. T　　3. T

Writing Drills;

Part A: Questions about the Model, p. 60.

1. The Job Fair was held at the Conference Hall, in the Centennial Complex.
2. college job-seekers

Part B: Questions about the Model, p. 62.

1. Korea Sale FESTA
2. traditional markets

Writing Tips;

A. Writing Skills; Practice 2, p. 65.

1. am
2. is
3. were

B. Grammar Skills; Practice 3, p. 66.

1. Where is the movie being played?
2. Information about earlier events is removed periodically.
3. I'm sorry I'm late, I got lost.

C. Collocation Drills by Subjects, p. 67.

(1) join, literacy, cram, doing, double, required, Communication, Aptitude

(2) get / get, withdrew, negotiated, exchange, protection, raise, restructuring, abolish

Unit 4 Travel Descriptions

Warm-up Activity; Practice 1, p. 78.

1. T
2. T
3. T

Writing Drills;

Part A: Questions about the Model, p. 79.

1. street vendors

Part B: Questions about the Model, p. 82.

1. the Paramount Pictures Studio Tour and Sony Pictures Studio Tour

Writing Tips;

A. Writing Skills; Practice 2, p. 86.

1. T
2. T
3. F

B. Grammar Skills; Practice 3, p. 86.

1. yet	2 also	3. affect
4. to	5. further	6. farther

C. Collocation Drills by Subjects, p. 87.

(1) in	peak	convenience
round	souvenir	wake-up
make	"Do Not Disturb"	

(2) broaden	boarding time	check-in
boarding pass	free	NC-17
seatbelts	license	

Unit 5 Resumes and Cover Letters

Warm-up Activity; Practice 1, p. 98.

1. T   2. F

Writing Drills;

Part B: Questions about the Model, p. 102.

1. English for Interpretation and Translation

Writing Tips;

A. Writing Skills; Practice 2, p. 105.

1. T	2. T	3. T

B. Grammar Skills; Practice 3, p. 106.

1. during, for	2. though	3. tallest
4. childish	5. historic	

C. Collocation Drills by Subjects, p. 107.

(1) upon	Fluency	with
from	Scored	in
Proficient	exchange	

(2) enclosing	schedule	discussing
position	challenging	qualifications
interest	with	

Credits

Unit 1 E-mail

p.13 https://www.freepik.com/free-vector/e-mail-concept-with-paper-planes_765773.htm#term=email&page=1&position=18

p.32 https://pixabay.com/ko/%EB%A9%94%EC%9D%BC-%EB%A9%94%EC%8B%9C%EC%A7%80-%EB%A9%94%EC%9D%BC-%EC%A3%BC%EC%86%8C-%EB%AC%B8%EC%9E%90-%EB%B3%B4%EB%82%B4-%EC%97%B0%EB%9D%BD%EC%B2%98-%EB%B4%89%ED%88%AC-%EB%B3%B4%EB%82%B4%EA%B8%B0-1454731/

Unit 2 Text Messages and Comments

p.33 https://pixabay.com/ko/%EB%A9%94%EC%9D%BC-%EC%A3%BC%EC%86%8C-%EB%A9%94%EC%8B%9C%EC%A7%80-%EB%B4%89%ED%88%AC-%EC%A0%95%EB%B3%B4-%ED%9C%B4%EB%8C%80-%EC%A0%84%ED%99%94-%EC%8A%A4%EB%A7%88%ED%8A%B8%ED%8F%B0-%EC%A0%84%ED%99%94-1903444/

p.42 https://www.reddit.com/r/funny/comments/944tc9/i_dont_mean_to_bother_you_but_could_i_get/

p.43 https://pixabay.com/ko/cms-%EC%9B%8C%EB%93%9C-%ED%94%84%EB%A0%88%EC%8A%A4-%EC%BD%98%ED%85%90%EC%B8%A0-%EA%B4%80%EB%A6%AC-%EC%8B%9C%EC%8A%A4%ED%85%9C-%EA%B4%91%EA%B3%A0-%EB%AC%B8%EC%95%88-%EC%BD%98%ED%85%90%EC%B8%A0-%EC%9B%B9-265125/

p.44 http://www.theargus.org/gisa_view.asp?no=1411

p.52 https://pixabay.com/ko/%EC%9B%8C%EB%93%9C-%ED%94%84%EB%A0%88%EC%8A%A4-%EB%B8%94%EB%A1%9C%EA%B7%B8-%EA%B2%8C%EC%8B%9C%EB%AC%BC-cms-%EC%BD%98%ED%85%90%EC%B8%A0-%EA%B4%80%EB%A6%AC-%EC%8B%9C%EC%8A%A4%ED%85%9C-265132/

Unit 3 News Letters

p.53 직접 촬영

p.55 http://www.theargus.org/gisa_view.asp?no=1245

p.56 https://templates.office.com/en-us/Employee-newsletter-TM06088944

p.59 http://www.hufs.ac.kr/user/hufsenglish/

p.62 http://kto.visitkorea.or.kr/eng/pr.kto

p.72 https://www.freepik.com/free-vector/business-brochure-template-with-green-geometric-shapes_1296191.htm#term=brochure&page=1&position=3

p.72 http://english.kca.go.kr/brd/m_11/list.do

Unit 4 Travel Descriptions

p.73 https://trawellblogging.com/contact/

p.75 http://english.visitkorea.or.kr/enu/ATR/SI_EN_3_6.jsp?cid=1630721

p.76 http://english.visitkorea.or.kr/enu/ATR/SI_ENG_2_3_1.jsp

p.79 http://english.visitkorea.or.kr/enu/ATR/SI_ENG_2_10.jsp

p.80 http://english.visitkorea.or.kr/enu/FOD/FO_ENG_2_1.jsp

p.82 https://www.visittheusa.com/experience/insiders-guide-hollywood

p.83 https://pixabay.com/ko/%EC%A7%80%EB%8F%84-%EC%97%AC%ED%96%89-png-%EC%B1%85-%EC%B0%BE%EC%95%84%EB%B3%B4%EA%B8%B0-%EB%8F%85%EC%84%9C-%EC%96%B4%EB%93%9C%EB%B2%A4%EC%B3%90-%ED%83%90%EC%82%AC-%EC%97%AC%EA%B0%80-2686802/

p.92 https://www.google.co.kr/imgres?imgurl=https://i.pinimg.com/736x/5b/d9/c8/5bd9c8711d4a34d936754868126f6329--photo-album-scrapbooking-scrapbook-layouts-travel.jpg&imgrefurl=https://www.pinterest.com/thressal/scrapbook-layouts-vacation/&h=575&w=542&tbnid=6D34fJiCdlD_kM&tbnh=231&tbnw=218&usg=__OP2pxjo-jqzbBEcQR7ea4crVUYA=&hl=ko&docid=qR6aQ2gACklQFM#h=575&imgdii=6D34fJiCdlD_kM:&tbnh=231&tbnw=218&w=542

저자 소개

최호성은
미국 인디애나주립대에서 영어교육으로 박사학위를 받았고,
현재 한국외국어대학교 TESOL영어학전공 교수로 재직 중이며
학생·인재개발처장을 맡고 있다.

유호정은
미국 애리조나주립대에서 영어 글쓰기교육으로 박사학위를 받았고,
현재 경일대학교 국제통상학전공 부교수로 재직 중이다.

이진환은
한국외국어대학교에서 영어학으로 박사학위를 받았고,
현재 한국외국어대학교 외국어교육센터 책임연구교수로 재직 중이며
외국어교육센터(글로벌) 교수부장을 맡고 있다.

THE ESSENCE OF WRITING 2
GENRE-BASED APPROACH

초판 1쇄 발행	2018년 8월 22일
초판 2쇄 발행	2019년 8월 27일
초판 3쇄 발행	2020년 8월 28일

지은이	최호성 · 유호정 · 이진환
영문 감수	Alice Julianna Yoo · Brian Hupman

발행인	김인철
총괄 · 기획	윤성우 Director, University Knowledge Press
편집장	신선호 Executive Knowledge Contents Creator
전자책 · 사전	장혜린 Contents Creator
도서편집	이근영 Contents Creator
재무관리	하누리 Managing Creator
발행처	한국외국어대학교 지식출판콘텐츠원 02450 서울특별시 동대문구 이문로 107 전화 02)2173-2493~7 팩스 02)2173-3363 홈페이지 http://press.hufs.ac.kr 전자우편 press@hufs.ac.kr 출판등록 제6-6호(1969. 4. 30)
디자인 · 편집	(주)이환디앤비 02)2254-4301
인쇄 · 제본	(주)케이프린텍 053)313-3673

ISBN 979-11-5901-373-7 14740 정가 10,000원
ISBN 979-11-5901-267-9 (세트)

*잘못된 책은 교환하여 드립니다.

HUiNE은 한국외국어대학교 지식출판콘텐츠원의 어학도서, 사회과학도서, 지역학 도서 Sub Brand이다. 한국외대의 영문명인 HUFS, 현명한 국제전문가 양성(International +Intelligent)의 의미를 담고 있으며, 휴인(携引)의 뜻인 '이끌다, 끌고 나가다'라는 의미처럼 출판계를 이끄는 리더로서, 혁신의 이미지를 담고 있다.

THE ESSENCE OF WRITING 2

GENRE-BASED APPROACH